GUIDANCE MONOGRAPH SERIES

Shelley C. Stone

Bruce Shertzer

Editors

GUIDANCE MONOGRAPH SERIES

The general purpose of Houghton Mifflin's Guidance Monograph Series is to provide high quality coverage of topics which are of abiding importance in contemporary counseling and guidance practice. In a rapidly expanding field of endeavor, change and innovation are inevitably present. A trend accompanying such growth is greater and greater specialization. Specialization results in an increased demand for materials which reflect current modifications in guidance practice while simultaneously treating the field in greater depth and detail than commonly found in textbooks and brief journal articles.

The list of eminent contributors to this series assures the reader expert treatment of the areas covered. The monographs are designed for consumers with varying familiarity to the counseling and guidance field. The editors believe that the series will be useful to experienced practitioners as well as beginning students. While these groups may use the monographs with somewhat different goals in mind, both will benefit from the treatment given to content areas.

The content areas treated have been selected because of specific criteria. Among them are timeliness, practicality, and persistency of the issues involved. Above all, the editors have attempted to select topics which are of major substantive concern to counseling and guidance personnel.

Shelley C. Stone

Bruce Shertzer

EXISTENTIAL THEORY FOR COUNSELORS

DAVID H. FREY
FREDERICK E. HESLET
CALIFORNIA STATE UNIVERSITY
AT HAYWARD

HOUGHTON MIFFLIN COMPANY · BOSTON
ATLANTA · DALLAS · GENEVA, ILL. · HOPEWELL, N.J. · PALO ALTO

ISBN: 0-395-200393

Library of Congress Catalog Card
Number: 74-11964

COPYRIGHT © 1975 BY HOUGHTON MIFFLIN COMPANY. *All rights reserved. No part of this work may be reproduced or transmitted in any form or by any means, electronic or mechanical, including photocopying and recording, or by any information storage or retrieval system, without permission in writing from the publisher. Printed in the U.S.A.*

DEDICATION

For our children
Anne, Joe, Tony, and Erick

CONTENTS

EDITORS' INTRODUCTION ix

AUTHORS' INTRODUCTION xi

1. *The Existential Matrix* 1
2. *Significant Persons* 11
3. *Major Themes* 21
4. *The Goals of Counseling* 33
5. *About Technique* 44
6. *Person Centered Assessment* 60
7. *Will and Transition* 73

GLOSSARY 83

BIBLIOGRAPHY 91

INDEX 97

EDITORS' INTRODUCTION

This monograph presents an approach to counseling and therapy which has been viewed by some as being very awesome and complete but by others as incomprehensible and hopelessly complex. The existential approach to counseling is indeed a highly complex theory. Its broad philosophical foundations, its difficult terminology, and its failure to specify clearly its activities are the source of much criticism. At the same time, existentialist thought has had a strong positive valence for those working in the helping relationships because of its aversion to fractionating the client in an effort to understand him, and because of its insistence that a holistic approach is the only feasible one which will permit understanding of the client's being. Virtually all counselors share with existentialists the beliefs that: 1) man is being and becoming through a dynamic process, and 2) man is a highly complex organism existing in relation to his environment and universe.

For many in the counseling field, explication of the existential viewpoint has been the problem rather than its basic wisdom, attraction, and comprehensiveness. David Frey and Frederick Heslet have waded through the morass of philosophy, theory, and terminology for the reader. They are to be congratulated for emerging from this formidable task with a manuscript focused on application and one which, without ignoring foundational theory, clarifies the existential view of man as it is applied in counseling. Both their humanistic bent and their desire for scientific confirmation show throughout the material. This is a rich and provocative resource for all practitioners of the art and science of helping.

SHELLEY C. STONE
BRUCE SHERTZER

AUTHORS' INTRODUCTION

This monograph was written with a distinct purpose in mind. Our intention is to give counselors and personnel workers an idea of how existential theory is applicable to them in their day-to-day work with clients. We tried, as much as possible, to center on the practical work setting while not completely undercutting theoretical and philosophical issues. Existential literature is heavy with works about the philosophy of man, the theory of human relationships, and the spiritual and philosophic basis for counseling and psychotherapy. We saw no need to replow that ground, but rather attempted to begin on this strong base. Therefore, this monograph has chapters about specific goals, technique, assessment, and termination.

These persons helped us: Lynne Frey who worked on the rough draft, Terry Robinson who typed the final copy, Derald Sue who gave us insights into writing, Tom Anderson who prepared the glossary of terms especially for this monograph, and of course the many students and clients who taught us and gave us something to write about. Thank you.

We are envious of authors who have specific and easily defined topics. Existentialism touches on philosophy, medicine, education, literature, politics, psychology, sociology and anthropology, and art. Moreover, there are thousands of persons who have influenced existential thinking. Our task was vast, especially when we had to compress it into one hundred pages or so. Something the Durants said helped us with this, and set the rationale for dealing with such a complex task. They said writing history "... is a precarious enterprise, and only a fool would try to compress a hundred centuries into a hundred pages of hazardous conclusions" (Durant, W. and Durant, A., 1968, p. 13). However, they said they must proceed.

So too do we proceed.

DAVID H. FREY
FREDERICK E. HESLET

1

The Existential Matrix

An Aggregate

It can be said that existentialism doesn't exist but existentialists do. How else can you explain the varied camp that houses Sartre the founder of the nausea school of French philosophy, Kierkegaard the pious Protestant cleric, Marcel the Catholic, Buber the Jewish philosopher, and Nietzsche who declared God dead? The litany of differences also includes Dostoevski the Russian author, Unamuno the Spanish poet, the German philosophers Jaspers and Husserl and Heidegger, and a whole series of therapists including the psychoanalytic Boss and Binswanger, the Gestaltist Perls, client centered Rogers, and May, Frankl, Moustakas, van Kaam and Laing.

Existentialists are a mixed breed which may include atheists, theists, philosophers, literary figures and men of practical and applied fields such as medicine, psychotherapy, and education.

While common themes run through the work of existentialists one is too often tempted to classify them beyond the boundaries of their real and shared likenesses. In many ways, these thinkers are more dissimilar than similar. Still, it is important to stress that each has remained an existentialist — at least in the elemental areas such as metaphysics — by centering on immediate tasks in order to validate existence, to define meaning, and to become committed. These outcomes and the processes used to reach them are central to all existentialists whether their work is writing, educating, thinking, doing art, or healing.

Existentialism is an aggregate rather than a mixture. Aggregates are loose collections of things or elements sharing the same space while keeping the character of each element. Each element is both an individual and part of the collection. If we go to the beach and gather small stones that attract our eye, we have an aggregate. Each stone becomes a part of the collection but keeps its own quality. Some may be fancy and others plain. Others may be colored or dull. Each is both an individual and a part of a larger group. But our attention is drawn to the individual stone. Mixtures, on the other hand, combine elements to form a more homogeneous product. Our attention is focused on the newer product. Suppose we take the stones and add cement, sand, and water. The concrete or the homogeneous product transcends the elements and we don't see sand, stones, cement, or water. We see concrete. In aggregates, the individual elements have power. In mixtures, the power lies in the bonds among elements.

Both in terms of style and history, existentialists have preferred aggregates over mixtures. They have been unconcerned that they have no "school of thought" and find it relatively easy to live with this ambiguity, often relishing the contradictions, rather than trying to resolve them. The student of existentialism is left with this set and has to select for himself, making choices as to personal utility and meaning.

Personal Investigation

We, too, have to make choices. We can center our attention on the rich literary and philosophical background of existential theory; analyzing such topics as the nature of man, or the differences between validated being and inauthentic being. We can focus on the psychoanalytic foundations of most existential therapy to show how the existentialists have humanized many traditional procedures. We can focus on anthropology and study the interface between contemporary man and culture. However, the choices must come from our experience.

We are counselors. We are not philosophers, analysts, or anthropologists. Our experience is in doing counseling, helping persons to work through issues regarding their educational, vocational, and personal development.

Our goal is to help the reader better understand something of what it's like to do existential counseling in settings that employ counselors (i.e., elementary and secondary schools, colleges and universities, and agencies). For the most part, these settings are not "ivory towers" but are designed to accomplish specific missions. Schools need to educate students. Agencies receive their funding because they serve a need such as the reduction of drug abuse, the rehabilitation of prisoners, or helping adults deal more effectively with their concerns. In order to help describe what it's like to do existential counseling, two parameters will be used to help make decisions about what to include and what to exclude; they are personal impact and tangibility.

Impact

Certain ideas and procedures have stood the test of time for us. They have been proved and strengthened through use and application. For example, we have used May's work on intentionality to understand decision making, Binswanger's *eigenwelt* to conceptualize self, the principle of "encounter" to define the counseling relationship, and Kelly's and Roger's writings as a base for phenomenological practice.

Rather than attempt to survey all of existential thought in so brief a monograph as this, we will select material that has had impact on us as persons and as practitioners. Others will have to write a comprehensive history and description of existential theory for counselors; for now, we much prefer to approach the task from our experience and values. Each person is unique and what we find impactful is also unique.

Tangibility

Philosophy and theory have had a most interesting public image. Many persons too often discount theory as so much academic fluff, something of little form and certainly of little use. This view is especially common in the United States where we have traditionally praised the practical man over the theorist. Still one does not have to look very deeply to understand that theory has been a potent and consistent force in the development of the world of nations and persons. Artistotle's scientific method has accompanied most scientists' experiments since the fourth century before Christ. Marxism remains alive in Russia, China, and Eastern Europe. And all of us have been educated by the pedagogy of the American pragmatists John Dewey and William Kilpatrick.

Theory is tangible. We can focus on the abstract and ethereal segments of theory and in so doing deny the concrete and particular. It's a choice of perspective. Counseling cannot exist except in relation to a counselor or client. Caring, love or hate, empathy, for example find expression in persons just as other theoretical principles are framed in real behavior in real persons in real situations. The test of Hitler's theory was Germany in the thirties and forties. The ideas of Aquinas are validated by the actions of the Thomists, and the approaches of Rogers, Perls, Adler, and Jung are realized by their followers in day-to-day meetings with their clients.

The point of all of this is that existential counseling is tangible and is centered in persons and places, using real data for concrete decisions. Perhaps this famous passage from Ernest Hemingway's *A Farewell to Arms* says it best.

> I was always embarrassed by the words sacred, glorious, and sacrifice and the expression in vain. We had heard them, sometimes standing in the rain almost out of earshot, so that only the shouted words came through, and had read them on proclamations that were slapped up by wallposters over other proclamations, now for a long time, and I had seen nothing sacred, and the things that were glorious had no glory and the sacrifices were like the stockyards at Chicago if nothing was done with the meat except bury it. There were many words that you could not stand to hear and finally only the names of places had dignity. Certain numbers were the same way and certain dates and these with the names of places were all you could say and have them mean anything. Abstract words such as glory, honor, courage, or hallow were obscene beside the concrete names of villages, the numbers of roads, the names of rivers, the numbers of regiments and the dates.* [Cited in Barrett, 1962, p. 44]

Thus, the true test of existentialism is on the firing line, in the world of real persons and events, and not in the world of ideas alone. For it is in tangible things that persons face reality and meet the challenge.

Definition

Before we can move on it's important to define what we mean by existential counseling. Some concepts have the quality of becoming almost opaque as to meaning. If we ask twenty psychologists to define the word personality, we may get twenty different definitions. So it goes for words like therapy, counseling, guidance, health, education, and existential. The nagging character of these words is that their meanings have to be defined constantly. Often each person uses such terms in a personal way, assuming that

---

* The passage is reprinted by permission of Charles Scribner's Sons, Publishers, New York.

others have accepted his idiosyncratic meaning. Rather than communication, the result is polite nodding followed by looks of bewilderment.

Existential counseling includes both a philosophy and practice that centers upon the existing person as he is emerging and becoming in terms of himself, others, and the world. Existential counseling implies that both the counselor and client are active partners in the developing process of making proactive decisions and implementations.

Elaboration of the key terms used in the preceding paragraph makes it possible to more fully understand our meaning. Existential counseling:

1. *includes both a philosophy and practice* — Hopefully what the counselor does matches what he thinks he is doing. There is a linkage between theory and practice. Existentialists are not interested in forcing splits between objective or practical reality and subjective or theoretical thought, but strive to work at a level which makes the subject-object or theory-practice dichotomy irrelevant (Kemp, 1971; Rosso and Frey, 1973).

2. *centers upon the existing person* — One starts with the client and not some *a priori* definition of him or his condition. Existentialists hold that existence is not determined by essence. Essences are immutable principles, truths, laws, or factors that stand above an individual's existence. Existence is the fact of presence. In the counseling dyad the meaning of existence begins with the fact that there is a person across the desk (May, 1960). Sensitivity to the fact of existence focuses the counselor's attention so as to reduce the common or universal and attend to the singular personal presence of the client.

3. *as he is emerging and becoming* — This phrase expresses futureness, growth, transcendence. Persons are viewed as constantly moving, dynamic systems; it's an organic biological idea, quite similar to Perls's thoughts on the necessity of organism-world contact as a condition of growth and maturity. Contact and interchange and incompleteness are also part of this idea (Raming and Frey, 1974).

4. *in terms of himself, others, and the world* — Self, others, the world describe the three interconnected modes of being and living, *eigenwelt, mitwelt,* and *umwelt* (May, Angel and

Ellenberger, 1968). Self in relation to self, self in relation to other persons, and self in relation to the physical world are analyzed by *eigenwelt, mitwelt,* and *umwelt,* respectively. Not only does each describe an important life domain, the order of movement from self to others to the world captures an existential preference.

5. *both counselor and client are active partners* — The encounter between persons is active, mutual, shared, personal, and honest (van Kaam, 1967). Energy is asked for and expected, and both persons are asked to commit themselves and their resources. "We" is the preferred pronoun, not "you" or "I" or "me."

6. *in the developing process* — Counseling is evolutionary, moving, flowing. It's not static.

7. *of making proactive decisions and implementations* — Proactivity involves surpassing present self and circumstances in order to gain something. It means reaching forward. It is self engineered, not conditioned or determined by forces outside the person. Proactivity assumes freedom and potency (Bonner, 1967). Decisions and implementations imply that persons can make up their minds to do something, that data can be gathered for rational action, and that something can be done or started.

In summary, this definition raises issues that are at the heart of existential thought and counseling practice. There is the need for authentic technique (the relationship between values and theory and action), the need for client acceptance, the need for an organic or growth-oriented concept of personality, the need to look at persons in relation to themselves, their social interactions and their world, the need for reciprocity between client and counselor, the need to view counseling as a process and not an event, and finally the need to place greater stress on decision making and implementation skills and strategies.

One more thing about definitions; definitions used existentially have heuristic value. That is, they are used to begin the process of finding out about something, not to end the process. Definition is the foundation and not the capstone.

The Place of Existential Counseling in the Matrix of All Counseling

Until quite recently, most counseling has been rooted in verbal interchange designed to treat disturbed "psyches" (words are used to help persons with their problems) (Harper, 1959). The advent of massage, body therapies, bio-energetics and the rediscovery of Wilhelm Reich may shift the balance from verbal treatment to treatment of the body as the reservoir of psychological pain; but for now, counseling consists essentially of two persons, a counselor and a client, talking with each other. This does not mean we have no concern for gestures, facial expressions, posture and other non-verbal messages. The point is, in counseling, most of the time and energy has gone toward understanding the verbal interaction.

How does existential counseling differ from other counseling? How does their verbal interchange differ from counselors holding other theoretical positions?

First, these questions are more complex than we may realize. We often tell students that if we had a series of rooms, each with the door open, some holding counselors and clients, and others holding friends talking, it would, we think, be difficult to tell who is counseling and who is just talking. There would be overlap between counseling and good human verbal interchange. In fact, persons who are good conversationalists, in the best sense of that term, have a real advantage in learning counseling skills. They have already mastered many of the skills needed by counselors. Furthermore, this little experiment might reveal the therapeutic quality of good verbal interchange, elevating friends as helpers and keeping professionals humble. Professionals do not necessarily hold the market on therapeutic communications.

Still, a deeper look indicates that counseling is different than regular conversation. It's more intense, more focused, more purposeful. It's more professional, more serious, and often more penetrating.

One way to answer the question about the differences between existential counseling and other methods is to investigate the interconnections among a variety of theoretical positions. This was done in a research project by one of the authors (Frey, 1972). The study yielded a four-celled model for describing counseling interactions (see Figure 1). The two dimensions in the model relate to the two major factors involved in counseling: process and goals.

Counseling goals are the expected outcomes of counseling. A goal is the result sought. Synonyms for goals are "try to do," "purpose," "aim," "objective." According to London (1964) goals can range from insight to action. Insight goals seek understanding of feeling, knowledge of inner self, awareness of self development and growth, and comprehension of intraperson and interperson dynamics. Insight goals seek an answer to the question, "Do you

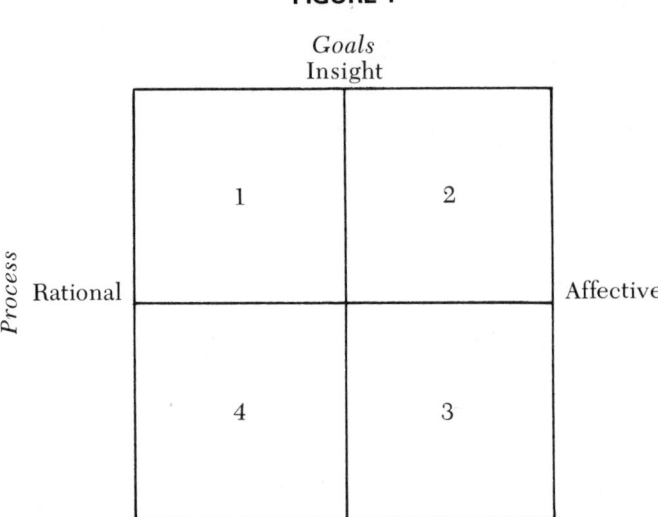

FIGURE 1

understand?" Action goals seek overt behavior change. Action, movement, performance, execution are preferred over knowledge and understanding.

Process is the activity in the interview; it's what is "going on." Patterson (1966) classifies counseling processes as either rational or affective. Rational process is characterized by reasoning, judgment, and logic. It tends to be planned, objective, and is sometimes impersonal. Affective process is feeling based, emotional, experiential, and tends to be personal, subjective, and spontaneous.

Using the goal and process axes as a base, we can now draft four types of counseling: insight-rational (type one), insight-affect (type two), action-affect (type three), and action-rational (type four). (See the drawing of the model, in Figure 1.)

Insight-Rational Counseling

Counselors operating within the sphere of this cell ask the client to "think with me so we can understand your concern." The process is rational and the goal is insight.

Albert Ellis is representative of counselors working under the insight-rational umbrella. Clients are thought to have faulty thinking processes and the counselor's task is to help the client to think straight.

Insight-Affective Counseling

This is the existential cell. These counselors ask the client to feel with them so they both can understand the client's concerns and dynamics. The process is affective and the goal is insight.

A number of theorists fall within this cell, among them, Carl Rogers, Fritz Perls, Victor Frankl, and certain psychoanalytic counselors. Perhaps Rogers best describes the affective-insight counselor. Rogers focuses on the existing person in both phenomenological and objective ways, seeking to experience with the client as they both move toward a more integrated and comprehendible understanding of the client's circumstance.

Action-Affective Counseling

This cell is theoretically perplexing since we have, so far, been unable to find theorists who are action and affectively oriented. This may be a function of the research to this point, but none of the traditional theorists analyzed, so far, fall within the boundaries of cell three. Perhaps, R. D. Laing (1967) and his personal-political system fits. Perhaps, the body therapies fit. Perhaps, Thoreson's (1972) behavioral humanism is an appropriate fit. Perhaps, nothing we know of fits, leaving someone free to develop such a system of behavior change.

Action-Rational Counseling

This is the behavioristic cell. It houses Joseph Wolpe, John Krumboltz, E. G. Williamson and others who ask clients to become involved in a scientific and systematic process so they can change their behavior. Counseling is seen as a problem in human learning and these theorists actively apply learning principles of one form or other to the solution of the client's concern.

On Models and Paradigms

As with all graphic maps, something is lost when we seek to identify the universal and common. It's a scientific fact that parsimony is bought at the price of individual complexity. So it goes for the model just presented.

The four cells simply describe various methods of counseling, doing this in a rather ordered and efficient manner. The deep and intricate elements of each position are lost. Therefore, we urge the reader to read more widely so as not to oversimplify what is in truth a very complex subject.

Summary

This chapter first indicated that existentialism holds many different persons, some in the arts and others in the areas such as medicine and psychotherapy. Therefore, an analysis of the field requires some focus, for without it, an analysis would be very difficult. Our analysis of existential theory for counselors uses personal impact and meaning and tangibility as the criteria for the selection of materials for inclusion in the monograph.

Existential counseling was defined as a method of helping clients develop: 1) by reducing the gap between theory and practice, 2) by centering on the existing person, 3) by viewing persons as developing systems, 4) by analyzing the client's personal, social, and physical worlds, 5) by viewing counseling as a reciprocal process, and 6) by entering into a moving, evolving process for making proactive decisions and implementations.

Finally, a four-celled paradigm was given for analyzing the interconnections among various theoretical positions.

2

Significant Persons

A Brief History

It's important to state that existentialism has European rather than French roots since the so-called existential movement has been so closely linked with Jean Paul Sartre. In fact, existential thinking has roots deep within nineteenth century intellectual life (Barrett, 1962). Soren Kierkegaard (1811–1855), a Danish cleric, first spoke of existential questions in his search to realize the truth of Christianity in his own life. His writings, so different from the reasoned Hegelian philosophy of his time, reveal an individual human personality struggling for existential self-realization.

Friedrich Nietzsche (1844–1900) achieved early brilliance as a scholar and developed an existential philosophy radically different from Kierkegaard's. He began his analysis with a confession of bankruptcy: God is dead. Nietzsche concluded that it's only through this confession that European man can sever himself from the umbilical cord of the gods and, therefore, begin to live the true struggle that he defines as human life. His philosophy is heavy and penetrating and served as a sharp tonic to cut through the sweet romantic sentimentality that was so common in his day.

Both Nietzsche and Kierkegaard represent the two major schools of existential thinking: the atheist and the theist positions. Nietzsche, of course, is the atheist, and Kierkegaard the theist.

However, it was in the German universities during the early twentieth century that existentialism, as we know it, first emerged. Three names from this period stand out: Martin Heidegger, Karl Jaspers, and Edmund Husserl. Heidegger and Jaspers are the founders of modern existential systems, since their work has formed the issues and models around which all others have worked. Husserl is noted for creating the phenomenological method.

As with many philosophical systems, existentialism remained within the walls of academia until events outside the university forced the philosophical system to deal with a social need. World War II was the event and Sartre was the evangelist.

Sartre and his friends and co-workers, Simone de Beauvoir and Albert Camus, used literature to convey their brand of existentialism to a France that had just had its foundations removed. Their despair coupled with an awareness of the power of the individual man to live (or die!) with despair captured the mood of post-war Europe and cold-war America. In fact, during the fifties and early sixties, Sartre and company were the intellectual "saints" of Bohemian communities, both in Paris and in this country.

Still, existentialism remains a varied mix and the popularity of the Sartre group only partially covers the contemporary scene. Others of importance include Gabriel Marcel, Nikolai Berdyaev, Miguel de Unamuno, José Ortega y Gasset, Martin Buber, and Paul Tillich, to name only a few.

Existentialists in the Healing Arts

We said earlier that this monograph was to focus on ideas that had impact on us as persons and counselors. Also, we want to focus on the more tangible ideas and processes in existential theory, especially those that relate to practice in schools and agencies. To do this we must concentrate on those who have had their feet in two places: the existential ground and the applied ground of counseling, psychology, education, and medicine.

The next two sections of this chapter will present persons whom we consider to have made major contributions to existential counseling theory. The first section will discuss the lives and works of men whose impacts have been rather broad. For example, they may have had contact with a variety of occupational roles and professional groups. Carl Rogers is one of these. Secondly, we will cite the work of persons whose thinking and writings have had a specific and direct impact on guidance and personnel services. Harold McCully is one of these.

Impact for Counseling and Psychotherapy

Ludwig Binswanger (1881–1966)

Binswanger was a Swiss physician and psychoanalyst who attempted a synthesis between Freudian and Jungian psychoanalysis and the philosophy and the phenomenology of Heidegger. Born in Kreuzlingen and educated at Zurich, he studied under Eugen Bleuler, one of the noted analyists of that time (Rychlak, 1973).

Like many young therapists of the day, he became disenchanted with orthodox Freudian points of view, especially the mechanistic elements. Binswanger believed that the existential position more closely described man and his plight and began to draft a theory consistent with his position. He first popularized the term *daseinanalysis* (Beck, 1963) which literally means the analysis of the *dasein* or the personal existence of an individual, with all the special meaning and complexities this entails.

Perhaps the most telling quality of Binswanger's position is that, even though he and Freud grew apart theoretically, their differences existed in a matrix of respect and friendship (May, 1960); this revealed in practice his ability to accept the existential ground of another in the context of a shared relationship. As you may know, this was rather unusual for Freud's disciples. Others, for whatever reasons, found it impossible to differ with the "master" and keep the relationship on course.

Binswanger's many books in German are currently being translated into English. The first entire volume devoted to him is *Being in the World* (1963). Another source of his thought is the book coedited by May, Angel, and Ellenberger, *Existence: A New Dimension in Psychiatry and Psychology* (1958).

Medred Boss (1903–)

Like Binswanger, Boss is a Swiss physician, psychoanalyst and author. While many of his efforts parallel the achievements of Binswanger, he strives for a more pure Heideggerian phenomenology (Rychlak, 1973). He has been especially lucid in his writings, describing *daseinanalysis* as a method for observing, researching, and understanding the client. The following quote reveals his reliance on Heidegger and the consequences of accepting existential frames of reference.

The psychotherapist who lets himself be thoroughly pervaded by Heidegger's ontologic insights will not be able to derive new words or phrases from the *daseinanalysis* for his psychopathologic descriptions. But he will win by it a tacit, but all the more reliable and all-embracing attitude toward his patient and the therapeutic process. If the therapist really understands that man is intrinsically a world-opening being in the sense that in him is the bright sphere of be-ness, comparable to a glade in a forest, all things, plants, animals, and fellowman can show and reveal themselves directly and immediately in all their significance and correlations, then he will have an unceasing reverence for the proper value of each phenomenon he encounters. [Boss, 1967]

Viktor Frankl (1905–)

Frankl's impact has been strong because he has been able to translate existential concepts into terms that can be used by many people, professionals and laymen alike. Born in Vienna, educated for both the M.D. and Ph.D., Frankl spent his early career as a staff member and then head of a neuropsychiatric hospital (Patterson, 1966). Even before World War II, Frankl was active in developing his own brand of existential analysis called logotherapy, which focuses on the spiritual and ontological underpinnings of behavior.

However, Frankl's existentialism received the supreme test when he was placed in a German concentration camp during World War II. Even though he suffered many horrible catastrophies as a prisoner, he describes the process of his suffering as a test and a process whereby he was able to create meaning. His existence was stripped of all unnecessary baggage, forcing him to come to terms with himself. He could choose to live or die. He selected life.

Perhaps, Frankl's *Man's Search for Meaning* (1963) should be the first book on existential counseling read by students. It is poetic, real, and makes the point in the context of human life rather than philosophic discourse. Among his other books are: *The Doctor and the Soul* (1955), *Psychotherapy and Existentialism: Selected Papers on Logo Therapy* (1967), and *The Will to Meaning* (1969).

Rollo May (1909–)

May can rightly be regarded as the chief proponent and practitioner of existential psychology and therapy in the United States. He was born in Ada, Ohio, and graduated from Oberlin College in 1930. After graduation, he worked in student personnel positions at Michigan State University, studied art in Europe, and finally returned to New York to study theology. Even though he was not interested in becoming a minister he was attracted to the ultimate questions asked in seminary.

After another period in Europe, May entered Columbia University to study psychology, eventually received the Ph.D. in 1949. Since 1950 he has worked as a lecturer, professor, editor, author, and therapist. Among his academic appointments are positions at the William Alanson White Institute of Psychiatry, The New School of Social Research, New York University, Mills College, Harvard, Princeton, and Yale Universities (Lirette, 1972).

Although he has written many erudite articles and papers, he is best known as the author of: *The Meaning of Anxiety* (1950); *Man's Search for Himself* (1953); *Psychology and the Human Dilema* (1967); *Love and Will* (1969); and *Power and Innocence* (1971).

May sees the existential movement as one that can overcome the subject-object dichotomy that has plagued Western thought since the Renaissance. He holds that existentialism has an affinity with psychotherapy because both are concerned with individuals in crisis. Existential therapy becomes most potent in crisis situations marked by anxiety, alienation, despair, and loss of selfhood. He further believes that other methods adequately deal with *umwelt* (the material world) and *mitwelt* (social interaction) concerns, but it is only the shared counselor-client encounter of existentialism that handles *eigenwelt* (a person's relation to self) problems (Reinhardt, 1960, pp. 246-249).

Carl Rogers (1902–   )

Perhaps no other person has had such influence on American applied psychology and education as Rogers. He never quits and his interests have been legion; they range from child psychotherapy, to research, to administration, to developing a personality theory, writing, becoming the archetype of the "counselor," championing the group movement, working as a philosopher of science, being a commentator of the current social scene, and analyzing contemporary marriage.

For us, his most significant contribution was humanizing the relationship between counselor and client. He first let other persons in on the dynamics of the interview from both ends, that of the professional and the client. Until Rogers first began to record his sessions, there was no real data as to what really goes on in counseling. The flip of his recorder button opened the way for a host of innovations. For example, research was now possible on the counseling process itself, not just the reports of what the therapist thought occurred.

Rogers is a product of the Midwest. He was born in Illinois, educated in Wisconsin, and eventually moved to New York for seminary training and a Ph.D. at Columbia in 1931. His professional career has included both clinical and academic appointments (Ohio State University, the University of Chicago, and the University of Wisconsin). Since 1964 he has been with the Western Behavioral Sciences Institute and then with the Center for the Studies of the Person in San Diego.

One of Rogers' pet projects has been the development of a philosophy of science that would allow a place for full humanness in psychology. He believes that an unsystematic humanism is doomed to failure, hence his drive to understand the interface between systematic and scientific approaches and the psychology of persons. In this work, he has been especially influenced by Michael Polanyi, the eminent English epistemologist (Coulson and Rogers, 1968).

Rogers is the author of *The Clinical Treatment of the Problem Child* (1939), *Counseling and Psychotherapy* (1942), *Client-Centered Counseling* (1951), *On Becoming a Person* (1961), and *Carl Rogers on Encounter Groups* (1970). He has written openly about his values, his life, his thinking. Should you want to read more, we recommend his autobiographical chapter in Burton's *Twelve Therapists* (1972).

Fritz Perls (1893-1971)

Perls's life spanned the time and experience of Freudian Vienna to Esalen. His experience was rooted in the earliest and most historic days of modern psychotherapy and the most avant-garde and current methods of treatment (Perls, 1969).

Perls was born in Berlin of a lower-middle class Jewish family, did well in grammar school, but became a "failure" at the *gymnasium* (the German secondary school). After a turbulent adolescence, sparked by an active interest in drama, he entered school to study medicine, reinforced no doubt by his experience as a Red Cross worker in World War I. In 1922, Perls attended the Berlin Institute of Psychoanalysis, was analyzed by Wilhelm Reich and supervised by Otto Fenichel and Karen Horney. Moving on to Frankfort and Vienna, he practiced psychoanalysis and became interested in certain existential groups operating in these cities. Still, he remained a classic analyst even though some of his ideas were beginning to change. It wasn't until 1936, in a paper he read in Czechoslovakia, that he realized his break with the more orthodox Freudians.

Perls fled Nazi Germany, first to Holland and then to South Africa. In 1945 he moved to New York, and then to Miami, finally to San Francisco in 1959. It was in California that Perls's ideas became fully mature and he began to become famous. This fame was accentuated by Perls's involvement with the Esalen movement from 1963 on. Perls died in Canada in 1971.

Perls developed a system of existentially based Gestalt therapy. The position aims to have the client become in contact with his environment in an organic, biological, total and creative way, facilitating increased self-awareness and personal maturity and autonomy. The Gestalt counselor reaches these goals by skillfully frustrating the client (forcing him to face the issues) in the present time or the here-and-now (Raming and Frey, 1974).

Perls's influence has been most potent through the work of his students and through the force of his own personality. Most who have worked with him credit him with being a master teacher as well as a therapist. He has, however, written over the years: *Ego, Hunger and Aggression* (1947), *Gestalt Therapy: Excitement and Growth in the Human Personality* (1951), *Gestalt Therapy Verbatim* (1969), and *In and Out of the Garbage Pail* (1969).

Abraham Maslow (1908–1970)

Maslow's influence on the field was certainly broad and strong since he was one of the first academic theorists to focus on the growth and self-actualized aspects of personality rather than on the pathological and reconstructive aspects. He was among the first to note that psychology and education had elaborate theories to explain abnormal development, but few if any to describe mental health and growth.

Maslow received the Ph.D. from the University of Wisconsin in 1934, holding over the years academic positions at Brooklyn College, Brandeis University, and a fellowship at the Western Behavioral Sciences Institute. At the time of his death, Maslow was a Resident Fellow at the Laughlin Foundation in Menlo Park, California. Among his books are: *Motivation and Personality* (1954); *Toward a Psychology of Being* (1962); *Religions, Values and Peak Experiences* (1964); and *The Psychology of Science* (1966). Recently two excellent summaries of his work have been published: Wilson's *New Pathways in Psychology: Maslow and the Post-Freudian Revolution* (1972) and Goble's *The Third Force* (1970).

His ideas are far-ranging, effecting work in vocational guidance, child development, and counseling. But perhaps his greatest contribution was to expand the concept and definition of the term psychology. Maslow believed that psychology should be: 1) more rooted in philosophy, 2) more humanistic, 3) more bold and creative, 4) more positive by focusing on the loftier possibilities of man, 5) more introspective and depth directed, 6) more person centered and idiographic, and 7) more concerned with creating health producing environments and cultures (Maslow, 1955, p. 27).

James Bugental (1915–   )

Bugental is most noted for his efforts in founding the Association for Humanistic Psychology. Further, he has been one of the leading translators of existential thinking for American practitioners.

Bugental received his undergraduate education at West Texas State Teachers College, gained a master's from George Peabody in 1941, and the Ph.D. from Ohio State University in 1948. While at Ohio State, he worked closely with George Kelly, who was then in the middle of developing his personal construct psychology. Bugental has held a variety of positions: teaching assignments at the Georgia School of Technology and the University of California at Los Angeles, private practice in Los Angeles and Menlo Park, California, and is currently attached to the psychiatry department of Stanford University medical school.

Among his major works are: *The Search for Authenticity* (1965) and *The Challenges of Humanistic Psychology* (1967).

Other Contributors

Certainly the men mentioned above are only representatives of those who have made significant contributions to the translation of existential thought for counselors. There are, for example: Adrian van Kaam, author and founder of the Institute of Man at Duquesne University; Gordon Allport at Harvard, who for over thirty years championed the study of the individual; R. D. Laing, the noted British psychiatrist and intellectual force behind the "radical therapy" movement; Clark Moustakas, the child therapist of the Merrill-Palmer School; and Charlotte Buhler, who initiated interest in the study of life histories and life goals.

Impact for Guidance and Personnel Services

After finishing a brief overview of the lives of persons who had broad influence on psychology and education, the authors now want to center upon men who have thought about and written for counselors who work in schools and other places where "guidance and counseling" rather than "therapy"[1] is the rule.

C. Harold McCully (1906–1965)

McCully was in a most unusual position to shape the character of guidance services in the United States by virtue of his leadership and administration of the NDEA training institutes sponsored by the U.S. Office of Education during the late fifties and early sixties. During the period from 1959 until his death in 1965, McCully's hand directed the philosophy and practice of many of the strong counselor education programs, requiring systematic rationales and improved performance. For example, many credit the wide-spread use of the supervised practicum, so vital to training, to his efforts.

He grew up in the Rocky Mountain region, worked with the Veterans Administration in one capacity or another, received the doctorate from George Washington University, and eventually went to the U.S. Office of Education (McCully and Miller, 1969). During his tenure in government service, McCully became interested in increasing counselor professionalization and in the philosophic foundations of counseling practice. He saw the relationship between existentialism's humane theory of man and the need in guidance for a philosophic skeleton upon which to attach the body of technique necessary to move guidance personnel from a technical to a professional status. McCully was among the first to comprehend counseling as a process of existential change, with the counselor as the change agent (McCully, 1965). He also developed a theory for viewing man in the helping professions drawing heavily on the thinking of Dostoevski and May (McCully and Miller, 1969, p. 131).

Yet, McCully's impact was not so much in his writings as it was in his position. Here was a government bureaucrat reading, thinking, and writing existential theory and applying the ideas to the practical concerns of counselors on the firing line.

C. Gratton Kemp (1905–1972)

Kemp was professor of education at Ohio State University and a major transmitter of existentialism for counselors. He was especially interested in the relationships among values, religion, and the therapeutic process.

---

[1] We believe that there is significant overlap between counseling and therapy. For the most part, the distinctions are accidental rather than essential. However, in the minds of many, there are different meanings for the terms and it is this differential definition that we use here in order to classify persons into two groups.

Among his major publications on these topics are *Intangibles in Counseling* (1967) and a paper published in a special issue of *The Counseling Psychologist* (Kemp, 1971) on existential counseling.

Dugald Arbuckle (1912–)

Like Kemp, Arbuckle is interested in the axiological and philosophical aspects of counselor education and the counseling process itself. Arbuckle worked in a variety of positions in education, eventually taking the Ph.D. at the University of Chicago in 1947. Since that time he has been a professor of counselor education at Boston University. He has been a prolific author whose major works include *Counseling: An Introduction* (1961), *Counseling: Philosophy, Theory, and Practice* (1965) and *Counseling and Psychotherapy: An Overview* (1967).

Carlton Beck (1930–)

Beck noted in his major text, *Philosophic Foundations of Guidance* (1963), that little attention had been given to the philosophy of guidance. His book traces the assumptions of guidance throughout history carefully examining the rationales for each school and stage of guidance practice. He concludes his text by presenting a detailed summary of the existential or the *daseinanalyse* point of view, recommending that it be used as the framework for all guidance work in the future. He stresses the fact that most guidance theorists have been devoted to problems of technique with few focusing on the assumptive base for guidance.

Beck is a professor of education at the University of Wisconsin at Milwaukee. Among his other works is an edited text *Guidelines for Guidance: Readings in the Philosophy of Guidance* (1966).

Summary

Existentialism has broad roots in the intellectual and academic life of nineteenth century Europe. Kierkegaard and Nietzsche first formulated the basic existential point of view, strongly influencing the later work of Heidegger, Jaspers, and Husserl. However, the movement gained wide public attention through the writings of Sartre and his co-workers Simone de Beauvoir and Albert Camus.

Binswanger, Boss, Frankl, May, Rogers, Perls, Maslow, and Bugental have been major forces in applying existential ideas to psychology and psychotherapy. McCully, Kemp, Arbuckle, and Beck have applied existential principles to tasks faced by counselors and personnel workers.

3

Major Themes

Existential Theory and the Humanistic Movement

Thus far we the authors have discussed the scope, definition and place of existential thought in counseling, looking at the complexity of various positions and the impact of significant persons. This chapter will continue this analysis by focusing on the major themes and ideas that have been associated with the existential point of view in counseling: first, the relationship between humanistic psychology and existentialism, then a description of phenomenology, the therapeutic encounter, and finally an analysis of themes related to existence and choice.

Humanistic psychology includes, but is not synonymous with, existential approaches. Too often one is said to subsume the other. As is well known, therapeutic psychology began in medicine and was embellished by empirical and laboratory psychology. At the heart of the relationship between the helping processes and the hard sciences is a mechanistic and deterministic theory of human personality. In such a theory, persons are said to be conditioned or driven by circumstances over which they have little control. For example, the behaviorist holds that it is the environment with its reinforcements that shapes man, while psychoanalysts say man is determined by unconscious forces operating within himself. For some fifty years (1900 to 1950) these positions essentially described most theoretical explanations of man and his nature. True, there were contrary rumblings in religion, philosophy and applied psychology, but the fact remained that a significant alternate model was not developed.

During the fifties and sixties existential philosophy and psychotherapy began to gain more attention. Moreover, psychologists and educators found it to be a way to fill in the gaps left when one uses psychoanalytic and behavioristic explanations and techniques. The humanists discovered existentialism as a ready-made philosophy that centers on the kinds of issues they were concerned about; namely, the non-determined, philosophical and idiosyncratic qualities of persons.

During these years the so-called "third force" in psychology emerged grounded in the more personal and phenomenological premises of existential philosophy. (Psychoanalysis is the first force and behaviorism the second force.) Bugental summarizes the major tenets of humanistic psychology by asserting that the humanistic psychologist:

1) Disavows descriptions of human functioning based wholly or in large part on animal studies.
2) Insists that meaning is more important than method in defining, designing and executing research.
3) Gives greater importance to a person's subjective experience over his objective behavior or action.
4) Sees a constant interaction between "science" and "application."
5) Is concerned with the individual, the exceptional and the unpredictable rather than seeking only to study the regular and universal.
6) Seeks that which may expand or enrich man's experience and rejects the paralyzing perspective of "nothing but" thinking.
[Bugental, 1967, p. 9]

He goes on to say that these qualities flow from a strong and active human valuing perspective, real interest and concern for the person himself.

Phenomenology

Phenomenology is a method of scientific inquiry that asserts that in the final analysis knowledge is based upon intersubjectivity, i.e., the approximation to objective agreement which persons can arrive at from the perspective of their unique phenomenal worlds. This means there is no knowledge unless "I experience it and record it from my point of view or personal frame of reference." Knowledge starts with and springs from the person (Rychlak, 1973).

Edmund Husserl (1859–1938) is called the father of phenomenology, having first designed and articulated its systems and principles. Furthermore, his methods of inquiry proved to be well suited to the questions asked by existentialists such as Binswanger, Rogers, and May. Its premise that we begin our investigation with "your" experience and not "my" interpretation of it was so congruent to their philosophy and mode of operation. So the force of phenomenology was to elevate the client's perspective and point of view to primacy within the counseling dyad; counselor and client began to share more equally in the process.

Rogers' (1942) client-centered therapy and the writings of Snygg and Combs (1949) did the most to popularize phenomenology for practitioners in this country.

While the informal position that "we begin with your experience" is universally accepted by all existential counselors, there are many differences regarding the validity of the formal stances of Husserl, Combs, Snygg, and others; this is especially true regarding the question of determinism and freedom. In the formal case, a person's behavior is said to be totally determined by his phenomenological field (the private environment that impinges on the self), making freedom impossible. As in the behaviorist position, the environment determines behavior. In one case, the forces are idiosyncratic and unique and in the other they are overt concrete situations and events. However, both determine behavior and nullify free choice (Beck, 1963).

As with many influences on the existential position, the lines of phenomenological influence are tangled and indirect. The phenomenological perspective had a great deal to do with countering positivistic and mechanistic methods of investigation, creating in its place a more personal method. Still, many disagree as to how the method should be employed and the degree to which our experience, personally perceived, limits our freedom. Sahakian (1969) lists a few differences between phenomenology and existential analysis:

1) Existential analysis does not restrict itself to the investigation of states of consciousness but takes into account the entire structure of existence of the individual.
2) Whereas phenomenology has emphasized the unity of the individual's inner world of experience, existential analysis em-

phasizes that one individual may live in two or more sometimes conflicting "worlds."

3) Phenomenology takes into account only immediate subjective worlds of experience. Existential analysis strives to reconstruct the development and transformations of the individual's "world" or conflicting "worlds." Binswanger stressed the fact that this study implies a biographic investigation conducted according to psychoanalytic methods. [Sahakian, 1969, pp. 255–256]

Thus, existential analysis differs from phenomenology in that it operates in a larger sphere.

The Encounter

To pick up on one of Sahakian's points, the existential relationship in counseling takes into account the entire structure of the individual. Since counseling involves two persons — the counselor and client — there are two entire structures to deal with and understand. This duality of interaction is the heart of the encounter.

van Kaam says:

> When we try to understand what counseling or psychotherapy really is, we should see it as primarily a human encounter. What is a truly human encounter? Everyone senses immediately that an incidental crossing of someone else's path cannot be called a human encounter. It seems that an authentic human encounter always implies that I am at least for some moments totally present to a person, that I am fully with him. In a true encounter I participate in the personal existence of another for whom I really care. To participate means literally to *take part in*. Encounter entails thus that I share the life of the other, the existence of the other, his way of being in the world. [van Kaam, 1967, p. 21]

Since the encounter between counselor and client is complex and rooted in the unique interaction set by time, place, and personality, across the board definitions of the process usually fall short. Definition is difficult because the encounter is personal and singular. It is very difficult to generalize from such data. Still there are certain qualities that can be extracted from a series of positive counseling relationships. Keep in mind that the following definitions spring from our experience and are indeed a puny attempt to describe the energy, reality, and humanness existing in a potent encounter.

The encounter is mutual. Without a commitment from both the helper and the one helped, no progress can be made. The encounter like any productive human interaction is reciprocal. It takes two persons willing to open themselves to each other. Such close and open interaction cannot be manufactured by either party but evolves in an atmosphere of freedom, sharing, and expanded awareness. "One cannot be compelled to be helpful or to receive help because the very force precludes 'helpfulness.' Duress tears at the fabric of understanding and creates mistrust rather than bringing about improvement" (Shertzer and Stone, 1974, p. 7).

The encounter involves contact. Unless contact is made through shared participation in the same space field, time field, and person field, rapport is less likely to occur. Contact means "my being *present* with you and you being *present* with me." Contact occurs on all levels: verbal, non-verbal, cognitive, affective, psychological and physical. In a very real sense contact is touching. As we all know, touching — a lover's pat, a warm hand shake, or a repelling push — intensifies communication at all levels. There is reason to believe that many human problems are caused by the simple failure to make contact or touch others. It's the paradox of our time when we can bounce messages off Mars, but find it harder and harder to send a clear message to our closest associates.

The encounter focuses on the moment. The present is more important than the past or the future. The encounter focuses on the "here and now." Fritz Perls discusses the "now" by using the Zen statement: *Nothing exists except the here and now.* He goes on to say:

> What is buried in the word now? How come it takes years and years to understand a simple word like the word now? If I play a phonograph record, the sound of the record appears when the record and needle touch each other, where they make contact. There is no sound of the before, there is no sound of the afterwards. If I stop the phonograph record, then the needle is still in contact with the record, but there is no music, because there is the absolute now. If you would blot out the past, or the anticipation of themes three minutes from now, you could not understand listening to that record you are now playing. But if you blot out the now, nothing will come through. So again, whether we remember or anticipate, we do it *here and now.* [Perls, 1969, p. 41]

The encounter is affectual. Encounter is partially defined with words like intense, fearful, deep, joyous, loving, hateful, satisfying, upsetting — words ranging across the total repertoire of human emotions. Encounters have a directed and intense feeling tone, those qualities that make counseling different than regular dyadic communication. To be more specific, mutuality, contact, and the "here and now" release a flow of feeling in both counselor and client. Moreover, the release of feeling, negative or positive, is valued and supported.

The encounter is a process. The encounter changes over time. It assumes there will be time to deal effectively with each other within a sequence of activities. The encounter is not an event but a series of events. The encounter is conceived as having a beginning, a middle, and an end, implying movement from beginning themes through intermediate activities on to conclusion.

The encounter is human. Theorists who describe the counseling relationship find it to be real, deep, open, and unconditioned. They find it to be intensely human. Attention is directed to the most personal aspects of life and personality, not to those set by role expectations. For example, if I talk with Tom, the sophomore, my interest is in that within Tom that makes him to be himself (the Tomness) and not that which is sophomoric. He's Tom, the student, not the student Tom.

Existence

Existence and choice are the two major themes of existential counseling. Existence is a term that has the richest connotations, calling us to consider the very foundations of our lives and the lives of our clients and friends. Existence centers upon the fact of our life, our feeling, the awareness that we are real.

Dasein

First of all there is the real and material fact that we are here, now, present in one place. The concreteness of this awareness in ourselves and others is the consciousness of *dasein*. It's a ringing out and calling forth the fact of our existence. It is an act of stating we "are" with all that entails, including our past, present, and potentialities. *Dasein* is an active and creative presence, the process of realizing the fact of our life.

Being and Non-Being

Persons, in existential theory, are condemned to constantly commit themselves to life or death; to generate through themselves the principles of their own life. In its ultimate form this condemnation asks that we deal with and resolve the greatest question of all: Do I make something of it or do I commit suicide? The decision of course can end with life (being) or with existential or real death. Real death means just that, the body ceases to function. Existential death, on the other hand, means existing by withdrawal, passiveness, despair, and futility.

Anxiety

Living persons experience anxiety. It is the price of being. It is the price of constantly facing the decision to live or die. Existential anxiety is, however, viewed as a positive driving force in the lives of persons. It feeds change and growth. Neurotic anxiety growing from fear and withdrawal, on the other hand, is a negative force; it leads to psychological dry rot. Not only is existential anxiety the price we pay for being, it is also its reward. Some counselors often have difficulty in grasping this since, at times, the client's cure appears worse than his illness. For them it's difficult to see how there can be growth and honor in valid anxiety and pain.

Death

Until quite recently, the topic of death was largely ignored and denied by counselors and educators. Still, the fact remains, especially from an existential point of view, that death is the surest statement of non-being. Also, centering on the fact that our lives, as we know them, will not go on forever gives one a sense of time within which to create meaning. Choices become exaggerated because we begin to realize that we don't have an unlimited number of choices to make or unlimited time in which to make them. Life stands out in heavier relief because of an awareness of death.

Pain

Pain is natural and expected. Unlike some other therapies existential counseling anticipates and receives client pain as a natural and regular ingredient for counseling. Pain by itself is not necessarily pathological; it is seen as part of the client's life. Perhaps it becomes the barometer of the client's circumstance, his struggle with the fact of his being.

Some pain and suffering is imposed from a harsh society or severe physical environment and other pain comes from within, created by the sufferer. Perhaps the following quote from Wheelis makes the point.

> We have not far to look for suffering. It's in the streets, fills the air, lies upon our friends. Faces of pain look at us from newspapers, from TV screens. We know them: black man swinging in the warm wind, sealed cattle cars rumbling through the bitter cold, the glare of Auschwitz at midnight, the sweet smell.
>
> And then there's always the suffering inside. But that's different. It may be very bad, this private misery but different.
>
> For many people pain is imposed, there's no escape. It may be impersonal, unavoidable, as by fire, flood, cancer; or man-made, as in

wars, sack of cities, rape of girls. Victims still have choice; there's always a little corner of freedom. They may throw spears at the bombers or bow in prayer, may curse or plead; but they may not choose to suffer or not suffer. That choice has been foreclosed. Starving blacks of Biafra scrounge for rats; Vietnamese children with melted flesh wander homeless, orphaned, across a lunar desert.

Many of us have never known this kind of misery, have never felt a lash or clubs, never been shot at, persecuted, bombed, starved — yet we suffer too. Wealth and intelligence and good fortune are no protection. Having had good parents helps but guarantees nothing; misery comes equally to high born and low, comes with the gold spoon, to prince and princess and ladies-in-waiting, to groom and gamekeeper, to the mighty and humble. We feel our suffering as alien, desperately unwanted, yet nothing imposes it. We eat, often exceedingly well, the roof over our head is timber and tile; we know deep carpets, thin China, great music, rare wine, a woman looks at us with love; we have friends, families; our needs are met. In some way, unnoticed, unknown, we must elect our suffering, create it. It may be quite intense.*

Joy in Living

It's not all pain, death, heaviness. The alternative is the joy and satisfaction that comes with knowing one is deeply committed to and living a full and productive life. To be sure, there is joy and satisfaction in this.

Existentialists, however, know that suffering is real and strive to find meaning and satisfaction in reality, in the suffering that is real. Any other path to an enriched existence is a sham. True joy is said to be found in the tested life, in the real human situation.

The Search for Meaning

Frankl's logotherapy states that a man's plight does not necessarily stem from "illness," but rather comes from his puny attempts to create meaning in life — to answer the questions, What am I here for? What am I to do? Frankl believes that life can be made meaningful in three ways: "First, through what we give to life (in terms of our creative works); second, what we take from life (in terms of our experiencing values); and third, through the stand we take toward a fate we can no longer change" (Frankl, 1967, p. 15). Meaning is found in the decisions and actions made.

In a sense, meaning must be imposed from within the person. We can't buy it, steal it, or seduce it; but we can look within ourselves for validation. The battleground is within the territory of our minds and bodies, nowhere else.

* Reprinted from *The Desert* by Allen Wheelis © 1969, 1970 by Allen Wheelis, Basic Books, Inc., Publishers, New York.

Being in the World

Existential counselors seek to participate with the client as he "is-in-the-world." Binswanger was most lucid in his analysis of this thought, suggesting that a person's existence can be best analyzed through his relations: through his *umwelt* (the person's interchange with the biological and physical world, the world of things and nature); through his *mitwelt* (the shared world of social relations including friends, co-workers, loved ones); and through his *eigenwelt* (the world of "I," the face-to-face meeting of the person's self with himself). Personal existence then occurs in three ways, three modes, each needed if we are to understand and participate in the life of another.

Moreover, the participation with another is not a static intellectual involvement only, but entails a more complete sharing of data. The sensing of the person's world is complete; complete with the fears, the joys, the sounds, the smells, the tastes, the sights of the client's life. How can a counselor, for example, begin to help an urban ghetto black student if he has no feeling for the client's physical environment, his society, his self?

The client's "being-in-the-world" is not still but dynamic. So, too, is the sharing of that world.

Authentic Awareness

Existentialists want to exist in the "center," not on the edge of things. Centering requires being against the accidental, the peripheral, the unessential. In the counseling situation, it means striving to know what is truly going on within ourselves and within others, to cut through the rhetoric, listening with intense awareness to the real and sometimes hidden messages within ourselves and our clients.

Authenticity demands a focus on, or the ability to direct our energy toward, the essential. Also, it is an act of courage. There's valor in authentic perception and a spirit of daring in acting upon our sense of what is authentically true. Authenticity implies correct and precise perception of self and other, including the courage to act in accordance and in rhythm with things as they are in truth.

Choice

At the core of existential counseling is choice. At the most elemental level, choice entails life or death decisions and at other levels includes choices among life styles, educational patterns, vocations, social patterns, and so on. The counselor's task is to be mid-wife at the birth of the decision, to help it along and foster its growth and development.

Freedom

Just as persons are condemned to life, they are also condemned to be free. There are no *a priori* definitions of what persons should be or become. But they are asked, by life, to live with the ambiguity and anxiety imposed by freedom. Again, at the base of this is the reality of open and free choice; we can know the alternatives, select among them, and commit our resources (our power) toward implementing choice.

Freedom is a two-edged sword, one edge is liberty, the second is responsibility. We can't have one without the other. In choosing, we necessarily commit our energy to the selected alternative. The chosen thing or act draws our resources and focuses our attention on the chosen; the force is with this alternative rather than the alternatives not elected. There is an imperative to confirm the decision and act on it. Responsibility, then, entails following through on the choices made, flowing with the natural vitality that occurs when we elect to direct our attention toward the chosen alternative.

Intentionality

May (1969) and Wheelis (1958) were among the first modern psychologists to think through the process of making existential choices in contemporary society. They considered the concepts of will, potency, and intentionality. Intentionality is different from intending; it is more basic and is at the foundation of the human experience. It means a person's ability to focus his attention; it is the power to perceive something psychologically; it entails the ability to intend; it involves an in-taking of the perceived object; it is an active reaching out and engulfing activity.

The interesting thing about intentionality is that it builds bridges between the person and the object (in more philosophical terms, it removes the block between subject and object). Not only is the intender changed by intentionality, but the object elected also is made different. May says that a house is "truly" different for the carpenter, the artist, or the real estate salesman. In directing his attention to the house the carpenter "changes" the house to mitered angles, Douglas fir, and a certain construction technique; the artist sees the form, the color, the asthetic elements; and the salesman sees the tax base, the price, the sales appeal. For each, the house is truly different.

Will

Stated very simply will means making "I will" or "I can" statements. It combines with and embellishes intentionality in the choice-making process, and carries it one step further.

In counseling, the act of willing first entails the focusing of attention on alternatives, and secondly framing statements that commit one to the elected alternatives. For example: "I *will* go to the state university," "I *will* enter the discussion group," "I *will* drop algebra and select an easier class," "I *can* complete my assignment," "I *will* love you," — the list of willing statements clients make are endless.

Willing is an active, reaching for, potent activity, tapping the base of personal power and human potency (Frey, 1971). It has helped us to understand the process of will by conceptualizing it in terms of power, politics, and potency: the power to make decisions and act upon them, the power to change. Corsini (1971) caught the spirit of potency when he described his concept of an ideal group counseling leader.

> My ideal group leader is well-rounded, well acquainted with the arts and sciences; he is at the same time adventuresome but cautious; and he has deep feeling for people and the capacity to drive them forward. I see Rogers as being this kind of person. George Bach, so different from Rogers; Albert Ellis, so different from both; — to mention people I know fairly well — all, fit this description. If they weren't on the side of good, they could be pretty mean for they are all so powerful in their various ways. I don't see the group leader as a gentle risk taker. He is a passionate person who gives of his all. In the heat of the fray he may — and I know I have — go past the boundary of normality — so eager and so passionate is the group leader in his task. The group leader who is really effective leaves part of himself behind. He is just not an orchestra leader; he is a playing coach. [Corsini, 1971, p. 29]

Self Definition through Commitments

If we see our lives as a series of choices, each one adding to our characteristics and personality we can visualize how we are the product of our choices. We are our commitments. We choose to take humanities — we enter the world of humanities and its influences; we choose to get married — we enter the world of marriage and its influences; we have children — we become parents and experience parenting; we take up sailing — we become exposed to and a part of the world of sailors.

Summary

Existential theory has been a strong influence on the development of humanistic or "third force" psychology and education, since it has provided the theoretical framework for the humanistic movement. Just as existentialism has influenced the humanistic movement, the phenomenological approach to science has strongly affected existential therapists. However, many existentialists disagree with the determinism of formal phenomenology.

Three themes may be used to characterize much of existential theory. These three themes are: the encounter, existence, and choice. The encounter, or the person-to-person meeting of counselor and client, accentuates the person's life and being, centering on such topics as being and non-being, anxiety, death, pain, joy, meaning, and authenticity. Movement and change imply choice — resolving problems with freedom, intentionality, will, and commitment.

4

The Goals of Counseling

An Orientation

The behaviorist would have some difficulty with the themes which were presented in the last chapter (Skinner, 1971); he would note that these ideas are too mythical and remote to ever be useful in practical situations; ontology is just too irrelevant. The more philosophical counselor would applaud the spirit of the existential themes, stating that it's about time American education and psychology turned to the "real" aspects of the human personality. The philosophers are often heard to say that American counseling is too concerned with technique and not concerned with the ultimate purpose of the therapeutic involvement.

In general, the philosopher is correct; it is true that we think about our procedures more than our expected results. This seems to be a function of the American fascination with technical matters, partly a function of the fact that many goals and themes are difficult to define, and partly because we consistently seek validation for our techniques within the interview. The behaviorist's point is also valid. If the existential themes are no more than mythical abstractions, then of what practical use are they?

The existentialist's task is to isolate themes and goals that truly cover the human part of the human condition while striving to make the abstract specific, tangible, and concrete. It might be said that the existentialist hopes to find specific application of themes that all people experience as truly human, i.e., anxiety, choice, the fact of being, and death.

The existentialist's task in counseling is to begin with the fact of a person, to experience with him the individual quality and character of his life, to focus upon the human themes occurring in the life, and to specify and work through real life applications and implementations.

Of course, all of this takes place in a very complex matrix made up of counselor values, client values and goals, and institutional expectations. In this chapter we will first describe some of the forces within the counselor, client, and societal matrix that influence goal setting behavior. Secondly, we want to present some goals briefly that are common to all counseling, regardless of theoretical orientation, and then to focus specifically on certain existential goals.

Forces Within the Counseling Matrix

Figure 2 illustrates the manner in which various forces influence the direction a given counseling encounter may take.

The Goals of the Client

There is sometimes slight correlation between initially stated client goals and the goals that eventually emerge as the counseling process matures. This often happens for one of two reasons. First, clients are often unable to specify any concrete expectations. They just know in some vague way that, "Something's wrong," "Things don't make much sense," "School doesn't mean much anymore." The energy to initiate counseling is there, but it's vague and unspecified.

Secondly, clients sometimes come with such specific goals that to center on these alone would make actual counseling almost impossible. "Tell me how to pass Professor Wilson's Engineering 783." "Get Mr. Combs, my English teacher, off my back." These goals, although very real and sincerely sought, must be considered in a larger arena if the counseling is to go further than just information giving or administrative action. In themselves, these goals do not allow enough latitude for explanation and analysis.

Figure 2 shows how the client forces (in-puts) move from the

FIGURE 2

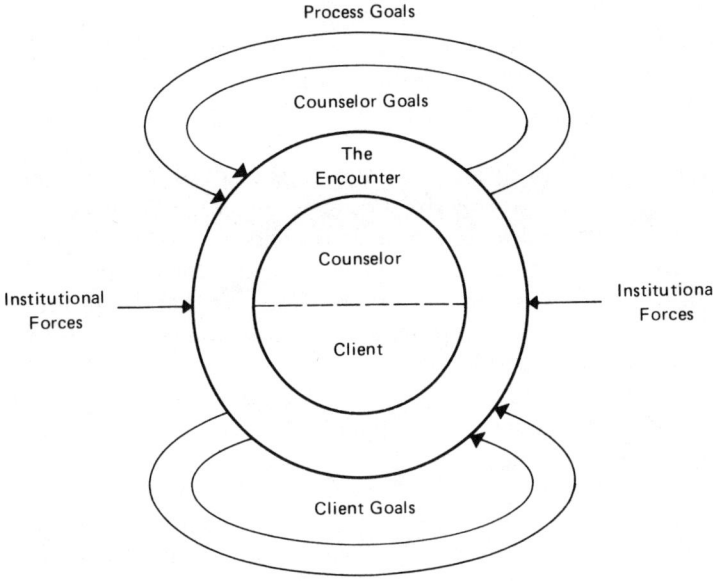

client to the counselor, certainly influencing the process and eventually coloring the goals of counseling. The forces can be vague, specific, normal, pathological, educational, vocational, information seeking (or giving), and so on.

The counselor's job is not to limit the in-put, but to become mutually involved with the client in extracting, analyzing, and working toward shared goals. (Note that we are stressing the mutuality of the goal determining procedure.)

Too often, counselors accept a client's neurotic goals as the ones to be sought, or worse, they turn the client's goals into goals they prefer. We recall one counselor who thought persons with vocational concerns were masking psychoanalytic (sexual!) difficulties and consistently shaped the relationship so as to move from the vocational to the "deeper" issue. In many vocational cases, repressed sexuality may indeed be an issue, but this goal is never sought by theoretical fiat alone. It's just not that simple. Successful encounters consider goals ranging up and down the ladder of intensity and abstraction. Persons often do say what they mean and there is no necessary reason to look for hidden agendas. Nevertheless, a sensitive counselor will be open to new data and new evidence and will not close the way to different and emerging goals.

The Goals of the Counselor

The drawing in Figure 2 shows that the counselor's goals move from the counselor to the client in the same way that the client's goals affect the counselor. Counselor goal in-put can be thought of as coming from two sources, the counselor as a professional and the counselor as a person.

The counselor as a professional brings a set of learned attitudes and values to the relationship. These values are usually common to all counselors; they include the acceptance of certain ethical codes, standards of operation, and professional traditions and mores. For example, most counselors believe their job entails the reduction of psychopathology and the enhancement of human growth and development.

Still, the counselor as a person remains in the encounter with all his strengths, weaknesses, and biases. As a case in point, the counselor may need to see himself as a successful person and thereby need to direct the counseling so as to force the client to "perform." In these cases, the encounter exists as a means of validating the counselor's potency and not as a process for helping the client grow and change.

Moreover, the ability to tolerate ambiguity might also influence goal setting. This tolerance involves a willingness to exist in a state of affairs capable of alternate interpretation; feeling comfortable when all is not black or white or right or wrong. Low tolerance for ambiguity could force the counselor to put premature closure on the topic of selecting appropriate goals, thereby reducing the probability of eventually meeting the client's needs.

Likewise the counselor's interests and special missions are also present. Consider the special values of the counselor at a birth control and abortion clinic, the counselor who does college admissions work, or the radical therapist angry with traditional elements in American society. Certainly their values are evident in their work and most surely influence what they do.

More significant, however, are the deeper psychological needs within the counselor's personality, needs that often seek satisfaction through clients. The need may be for intimacy (friendship or sexual), hostility, or support. These needs, unless understood by the counselor, may shift the relationship's emphasis away from the client toward the counselor. The client is there to serve the needs of the counselor. When the counselor's needs dominate the encounter, the client's role shifts from the "helpee" to the "helper," negating the focus on the client's own growth. We are not saying that there should be no strong feeling within relationships. Rather, we are making the point that the counselor, at least in the interview situation, is there for the client and not the other way around.

The Goals of the Institution

Counseling as a profession is an institutionalized activity — some ninety-five percent of counselors work in schools, universities, or similar settings. Needless to say, what counselors do is influenced by the missions of these institutions. The institution pays the bills, sets the job specifications, and imparts its values. The institution exists, to many counselors' dismay, and certainly will not go away.

Social psychologists and anthropologists have been active in describing the interface between persons and institutions. One of the best such paradigms was drafted by Getzels and Thelen (1960) and is especially useful to persons employed in the educational milieu. However, our task here is not to prove that institutions influence us but rather to remind us that they do, in fact, color much of our behavior, even in counseling.

For example, government has had a strong hand in setting counseling goals. During the late 1950's counselors were asked to respond to the nation's need for more engineers and scientists. Counselors became the nation's best defense against the threat of Sputnik. Counselors responded by helping many students elect careers in science.

However, the relationship between the institution and the counselor has not always been so pleasant. In fact, the struggle has been long and bloody since many counselors have championed the rights of persons against the rights of the group. This stance is indeed worthy of praise, but it's also easy to take the simplistic view that all institutional forces are negative and that all other professionals, i.e., teachers and administrators, do not care for the individual. This simplistic position pits counselor against teacher and principal and certainly specifies the kinds of goals set.

Aubrey speaks directly to this point.

> Maximizing the freedom of the individual while not destroying the goals of society is not a new problem for the field of education, nor is it the isolated concern of only the existential view of counseling. It will benefit children little to perpetuate a running battle between counselors and fellow educators on the proposition that "teachers think in terms of the welfare of society as taking precedence over the welfare of the individual." This simply is not the case, and those embracing this view would do well to visit enlightened classrooms from time to time. Finally, the entire issue of individual freedom and societal imposition is not an either-or situation, easily resolved by joining one

side or the other. As educators living in an era of increased strife, it behooves us to settle differences without attacking one another on the behalf of children. [Aubrey, 1971, p. 848]

The point of this is to understand the interchange between institutional forces and counselor and client goals, hopefully striking some compromise that allows the person to become free within an existing institutional structure.

The Goals of the Process

If we look at Figure 2 again we see that the process folds back upon both counselor and client. The encounter as it moves begins to have its own energy that influences direction and action. The energy comes from the interaction of the three elements already presented; the client, the counselor, and the setting.

It is interesting to note that many natural things, like human relationships, produce their own interactive energy. Flour, salt, water, yeast and heat interact to form bread. So too do certain chemicals yield a compound that is different from its elements. Two straight lines cross to yield a third thing, the angle that happens when the lines meet. So too does a cell within a complex analysis of variance experimental design potentially generate the so-called interaction effect. And so too does the encounter produce its own effect.

The effect of the process is of course unique to the persons or elements in the encounter. Likewise, the influence on goal setting is unique, special to this client with this counselor. It is, however, a force to be considered and reckoned with.

Universal Goals

Existential counseling, like all other helping procedures and therapies, seeks the general betterment of man including the reduction of "illness" and the enhancement of growth. All approaches to some degree are in agreement about these universal goals. Mahrer (1967, pp. 259–262) analyzed the goals of specific theories — psychoanalytic, client-centered, behavioral, etc. — and arrived at a list of common goals transcending particular approaches.

Mahrer's goals are:

— Reduction of psychopathology — reduction of symptomology and neurotic defenses.

— Reduction of psychological pain and suffering — reduced anxiety, hostility, and meaninglessness.
— Increased pleasure — intellectual, physical and sexual fulfillment.
— Enhanced self-relationship — self-acceptance, internal directedness, self-comfort.
— Enhanced external relationships — interpersonal closeness, social commitment, greater social adjustment.

Existential Goals

The goal specifying and selecting processes are complex activities involving the forces present in counseling and general societal and professional outcome expectations. Most existentialists would agree with Mahrer's compendium, but would hasten to embellish it with their own brand and style. In this section, we want to pose these questions about existential goal embellishment: How do existential counselors face the issue of setting goals? What are some more specific descriptions of existential goals?

To answer these questions the following is a series of existential counseling goals, along with a short vignette describing each goal in terms of school counseling, vocational guidance, or college student personnel work. The goals used were first articulated by van Kaam (1967, pp. 145–161) in Mahrer's text on the goals of psychotherapy.

Openness to Authentic Guilt

The goal — The client learns to accept himself for what he is and to accept his weaknesses, taking responsibility for error.

The vignette — An elementary school counselor is involved in settling a fight between three sixth grade girls. Two of the girls, Mary and Pam, have been vying for the friendship of Judy. Mary has been especially vicious in her verbal attacks on Pam. She has been actively and truly destructive in her use of false rumors and lies to discredit Pam.

Through the work of the counselor and the other girls Mary sees that her lies hurt Pam deeply. Mary accepts her actions, takes responsibility for her behavior and doesn't push it off on anyone else. She doesn't feel punished nor forced into a false sorrow; Mary realizes that her sharp tongue has hurt Pam. She owns her behavior and in so doing provides a base for better relationships from then on.

Acceptance of a Dynamic Existence

The goal — The client views life as an unfinished process that is not totally understandable and sees himself living in this ongoing, ambiguous continuum.

The vignette — Max sought out a counselor working in an adult school because he was troubled about the hopelessness of his present job. Max is forty-six, a high school graduate who has had twelve different jobs since he was discharged from the Army in 1946. His jobs have been mostly semi-skilled and, for him, very dull. He asks, "What is the right training program for me to finally select the right career?" During counseling he begins to realize that he has twenty to thirty years of vocational life left and that the choice to seek further training may be just a segment in the ongoing pattern of his career. He elects to enter a two year program in drafting, but does so in an openended way, fully knowing that his broad interests may mean further change and growth as the years move on.

Faithfulness to the Infra-Structure and Flexibility Toward the Super-Structure of Existence

The goal — The client becomes aware of and trusts the unchangeable aspects of his personality, yet remaining open to those things he can alter.

The vignette — Steven is an eleventh grade Chinese boy whose interests are in literature, poetry, writing, and reading. His parents and his older brothers, themselves engineers, have been stressing a scientific curriculum for him; supporting their arguments with the fact that an Asian can't survive in a literary trade in this country. Engineering fits both the Asian and Anglo stereotype. Still Steven, deep down, can't change from his interest in the beauty of words to the appreciation of mechanical things. Even though the choice is very painful he asserts his true interests and commits himself to work this out with his parents and brothers, knowing both he and they will learn and change.

Liberation from Psychologism, Public Image and Scientism

The goal — The client becomes relatively free from external expectations and is not defined by theoretical or practical constraints.

The vignette — Margie is so upset that she begins to cry while talking with Mrs. Conners, her counselor. Last year when her parents were divorcing and went to family service she took a psychological test that had a "sexuality" scale. She saw her score on the scale; it was 85 and higher than any other scale. She didn't ask the family counselor about this but was sure she was "over sexed" especially since she has masturbated from time to time. Others must surely be able to tell and Margie is concerned about "what they think of me."

Mrs. Conners slowly and with empathy uncovers the details of Margie's story, interpreting the test scale more accurately (it doesn't necessarily mean "over sexed") and providing data on adolescent sexual experiences in a discreet and realistic manner. Margie begins to sense her body and sexual feelings are hers alone, that other's can't "tell by looking," and takes charge of her own experience and existence. She tells Mrs. Conners, "It was wrong to pay so much attention to that score when I knew I was okay."

Acceptance of Authentic Conflict

The goal — The client views the end of counseling as a challenge to live in a complex world where conflict is real. The client does not seek a calm and issueless existence.

The vignette — Lillie is twenty-seven, married to John, a student, and the mother of Randy, age four. In talking with Stan Rizzo, the placement worker at her college, she explores the conflicts she and John are having living with their roles. Both she and John want their marriage, both are striving, ambitious people, both want careers and a family. Each is deeply in love with the other. To say the least their present situation is complex; it takes a lot of energy, for example, just to frame out their weekly schedule. Lillie knows all of her goals are good: her family, her career, John, her ambition. Rather than reduce the anxiety generated from this she existentially commits herself (along with John) to work within the boundaries of her life. She is sure there will be times when the conflict will be intense. She, however, begins to see this as part of the process she and John must face.

Existential Honesty

The goal — The client learns to see things as they are, not needing elaborate systems for self protection.

The vignette — The counselor is asked to help the eighth grade teacher deal with the class's response to James, the editor of the weekly class paper. The paper's staff is angry with James because he has just not followed through on his part of the work, but makes quite a thing of being editor and boss.

The counselor attempts to resolve the issue with a class meeting. Initially the class unloads on James. He responds by blaming them for his problems. However, as the air begins to clear and he senses some support he begins to see how his irresponsible behavior has caused him this difficulty. As the group senses his concern and he theirs, his vision becomes clearer until the events in his mind match events as perceived by his peers. James senses the more relaxed atmosphere and real concern. He reciprocates by becoming more open and free in talking with the class and his teacher. Throughout the remaining sessions, James is honest both with himself and with his classmates, even though some tension still exists.

Existential Commitment

The goal — The client gives up his self-centered existence and puts himself at the disposal of the demands of life.

The vignette — Don is deeply depressed. He has failed three courses in his major, his girlfriend doesn't seem to be able to meet his needs, his parents stopped their extra financial support, and he hates his part-time job. The more he tells Dr. Vance about this the more sorry for himself he becomes.

"The world is letting me down," he says to Vance.

The times with Vance are particularly difficult for Don because Vance doesn't feel sorry for him and has refused to linger in the self-pity. The therapy moves at an uneven rate, according to the support or non-support Don gets from his environment. But he begins to realize that the potency for his life is within himself and not in the world. Life asks that he do certain things: be in school, love his friend, support himself. However, it's he who must respond to life not life to him. He's in control and has the power.

Acceptance of Oneself

The goal — The client views himself with respect.

The vignette — Annie is a five year old who just loves to finger paint. She puts the paint on the paper with abandon, moves her hands so freely, and takes pride in showing off her finished products.

She tells her kindergarten teacher that she likes to paint more than anything else. "I'm the best painter in the whole world." She does seven finger paintings that afternoon and six the next day. And she begins to learn how to do weaving that Saturday.

Summary

First, the process of setting goals occurs in the matrix of client needs, counselors' biases and methods, institutional forces, and the effects of the counseling process itself. Therefore, common goals must be viewed within the larger matrix set by these forces.

Existential counselors agree with the general goals of most other approaches to counseling and psychotherapy, but seek to embellish these general goals with existential points of view. For example, existentialists would add: 1) openness to authentic guilt, 2) acceptance of a dynamic existence, 3) faithfulness to the changing and unchanging segments of self and the world, 4) liberation from stereotypes and public image pressures, 5) acceptance of authentic conflict, 6) existential honesty, 7) existential commitment, and 8) acceptance of oneself.

5

About Technique

Technique and Encounter

Relating is not enough. We apologize for starting on a negative note, but we want to make our point immediately.

Some uninitiated counselors hold that the encounter between the client and counselor is the existentialist's sole technique. They say that the technical processes in counseling begin and end with the dynamic flow of interpersonal experience within the relationship. They hold with the position that technique is self generating; we need to do no more than be kind of heart, they say, assuming the most empathetic posture possible. They accept the simple charge "go relate."

Existential counseling has techniques. Granted, the helping actions taken by a counselor are rooted in the relationship and deeply influenced by his existential attitude. They center on the experiencing client, his situation and his unique existence. Still, the counselor has to know how to begin the interview, how to make reflective statements, how to provide a supportive climate, how to express his concern, how to use appropriate language, how to end a session and so on. The counselor's technical skills manifest themselves in the encounter; technical competence is enriched and embellished by the dynamics of the relationship but not created by it.

Perhaps an analogy will help make the point more clear. We have a friend who makes pottery. His skill is exceptional; his pots receive wide acclaim. When we watch him he is so unconcerned with technique but concentrates on the clay and himself. As the potter's wheel turns and his hands mold the clay the pot appears to emerge as if by magic. It appears as if he is in union with the clay and the clay itself makes the pot. Of course we know this is not true, he is a master craftsman. He has practiced long and hard to become that free within the aesthetic experience of making fine pottery. It would be just as fruitless to tell a ceramics student to just "do it" as it is to tell a counselor to "go relate."

Therapists and counselors who do existential counseling use a wide variety of techniques. Many of the European therapists use psychoanalytic procedures, i.e., resolving the transference neurosis, supporting insight, etc. This group includes Binswanger and Boss. Similarly many Americans who studied in Europe or who had traditional clinical training also employ some psychoanalytic methods. Those existentialists who were influenced by Rogers may use Rogerian techniques. So it goes for those who were influenced by Perls or Bugental or Kelly.

Like most things within the existential aggregate most are different but there is some similarity. So it is with technique. May (May, Angel, Ellenberger, 1968, pp. 37–91) presents six ways in which many existentialists are alike technically.

— Existential counselors are versatile and flexible, often employing a variety of procedures within an interview or across many sessions. They try to use what is appropriate to more fully understand and work with the client's world at a given point in time.

— Many existential counselors use psychoanalytic dynamics — transference, repressions — to focus on the client's existential existence.

— Technique focuses on the client's real presence in the client and counselor relationship. The client is not to be analyzed but his presence is accepted as fact and incorporated into the shared therapeutic encounter. Counselor and client are said to be "in-relationship" or "being together."

— The counselor avoids techniques that remove him from the presence of the client, techniques that impede "being together."

- Technique is used to facilitate the client's experience of himself and his situation. The aim is to have the client become more fully aware of his existence in the fullest meaning of that term. The experience is affective, cognitive, personal and interpersonal.
- Existential techniques focus on change and commitment involving direction, actions, acceptance of new orientations and perspectives.

Above all existentialists strive to maintain an authentic person-to-person relationship. This is their unique contribution to counseling and that which makes their efforts effective. Our point is, of course, that the authentic encounter in counseling involves a series of known techniques and that these techniques are not incompatible with the human encounter or counseling success.

Toward a Theory of Technique

Since the historical forces in existentialism have been philosophical and attitudinal rather than technical, there has been little concern directed to "practical" procedures. This has been due, in part, to the concentration on themes that were not adequately developed in other systems; for instance, the philosophy of man or the more spiritual and mystical qualities of interpersonal relations. Because these themes are more particular to existential systems, it is natural that a great deal of energy has focused on them. These topics had not been developed and the need was there.

Patterson (1966, p. 450) agrees that existentialists have developed the philosophical domain, but states that their procedures just have not been articulated. He says:

> It remains true that those who profess to engage in a form of psychotherapy that has been influenced by existentialism have not faced the problem of methods or technique. For if they feel that techniques must be subordinated and must not interfere with the authenticity of the relationship, they should be concerned with amending involvement with technique and with defining how they function in order to do so. Not only have they not dealt with the problem as a problem, they have not provided illustrations or demonstrations of how they function so that one could attempt to understand or learn their methods and procedures. These methods and procedures must exist and therefore must be given attention, unless the approach is to be considered as entirely intuitive.

What about Patterson's assertion? What about existentialism and technique? As much as possible we would like to contend with the problem of technique in this chapter, concentrating on the issue at the expense, if necessary, of a philosophical analysis of the relationship. Again, note that we too consider the encounter to be the most important and the primary force in existential practice. It's just that others have developed this topic and few have addressed themselves to technique. We want to build on the work of May, Rogers, Moustakas, and van Kaam, not negate what they say. Also, we are limited by the space and time we can give topics in this brief monograph. We choose to concentrate on the practical and technical, not the philosophical.

We are not the only authors to do this; Corlis and Rabe (1969) and Johnson (1971) have also contended with the issue of technique in existential practice. We recommend their works for the reader interested in gaining a surer sense of existential technique.

Technique Defined

Technique is what shows, what we see, how the person acts, what he says, what he does. Technique is overt, concrete, objectively observable action. Two "technicians" are, therefore, present in each counseling dyad, the counselor with his action and the client with his. Both act. Our analysis, however, will concentrate on the counselor's technical processes.

The counselor's technique is a function of his personality and the role he accepts as a helping person. The counseling process specifies that he accept a helping role and its corresponding behaviors. This is part of the commitment and contract he makes with the client, himself, and his profession. The counselor in the encounter, for example, will not make toast or go to a movie. In counseling, his action, his technique is focused.

The interaction between the counselor's technique and the client's technique determines the singular quality of each relationship. Their unique transactions are what makes one session different from any other. The reciprocal system of communication and interaction is what turns our attention to the "here and now" and to the singular presence of the client's existence. Interaction lessens the possibility that the interview will be ritualized. This interaction is set in the matrix of a counselor accepting a helping role in relation to the needs of another person. The personness, the individuality of the counselor and client significantly contribute to the real, spontaneous, dynamic character of the encounter.

Technique Begins with Client Need

Some twenty years ago, counseling texts and journals were filled with debate concerning the relative merits of directive over non-directive technique on one hand or non-directive over directive on the other hand. Professors and students talked long, sometimes heatedly, about the merits of their particular techniques, always with the assumption, "I can define my technique before the fact." Counselor training too often consisted of learning how to "sound like" the "proper" model. To be sure, this mimicry was not the intent, but it was just too easy to respond like the master than to respond as self in an honest relationship. Technique grew out of the need to model, to be correct, rather than the needs of the client. Technique gets its legitimacy from responding to the needs of clients, not congruence with some fixed model.

Understanding Before Technique

Kemp (1971) and Ford and Urban (1963) note that existential therapy places understanding before technique. Both contend that no existential technique is valid unless it is validated in a process directly centering on the needs of the client and an accurate understanding of his existence in the therapeutic situation. Kemp elaborates, "This is in the direct opposite of much of the current national emphasis. Customarily it is assumed that if the right technique is used, we can then understand the uniqueness of the counselee." This approach objectifies the client, denying the subjective, and limits the emerging character of the encounter. How can we begin to become free to make choices, to develop, if the client and counselor do not have access to the technical system within which they operate?

Understanding before technique implies that we can alter what we do according to our best judgment as to what will be effective. In addition, the counselor's attention is drawn to the moment and not to the maintenance of a therapeutic plan.

Technique Cannot Stand Alone

Counseling technique has no validity outside the two person interactive system. Again, technique springs from need, understanding and awareness of the counseling situation. These processes are inevitably locked together so that one (technique) becomes the hidden side of the other (the encounter).

Technical virtuosity, performing to demonstrate your knowledge or skill, has no place in existential counseling. How ridiculous it is to think about the virtuoso counselor "performing" without a participating client. Showy virtuosity keeps the client from his own therapy; the counselor gives a solo performance.

Technique is Flexible

Technique is never planned so tightly that the dynamics of the interview cannot alter what occurs. Technique is not rigidly premeditated. Two factors are present when we consider flexibility: anticipation and deep listening. Anticipation means doing your "homework." It means thinking and planning for what you anticipate in the next session. It might include: collecting occupational information, deciding to become more relaxed and less interpretive, reading an article about persons facing marriage for the first time. Anticipation means getting yourself ready to be fully present with the client through greater participation in his life experience. Deep listening involves being so in tune with the client's present state that we don't impose our anticipations on him. Since we usually cannot fully predict what we will see and hear we must become sensitive to new data and new shifts in emphasis. Note that we are not saying we should not anticipate and plan, just have the flexibility and courage to move with the client if the situation demands it.

Post-Hoc Definition

Likewise, technique is often best understood after the fact. What happened? is perhaps a better question than what will happen? Rigid anticipatory definition often restricts spontaneity and freedom in the relationship, necessarily limiting the ability to respond personally in the moment. Indeed, this is a fine line to draw between planning and remaining loose, yet the line is there and must be walked.

Technique is Not Stylized

Crapo (1971) makes a distinction between robotlike and ritualized technique and a more spontaneous, free-moving action. The counselor is stylized when he responds out of his needs for comfort and in a stereotyped manner. Stylized responses are generalized and not to the point. Stylized behavior prompts the counselor to emphasize smooth functioning, to avoid ambiguity, to rely on two or three fixed responses, and to "play it cool." Reliance on style minimizes the importance of the experience too often placing a premium on the ritual, the safe, the easy (Winthrop, 1966; Halleck, 1969).

For example, a client directs an angry, sharp, personal verbal barrage at his counselor. The counselor remains cool and says as if out of the text book, "You appear to be telling me you are mad." What a put down! The stylized response has stripped away both the impact and direct meaning of the client's statements. The energy was moving from client to counselor, the counselor refused it and dumped it back on the client. He, in effect, says, "Keep your anger, I can't deal with it."

Other examples of stylized behavior might be forced eye contact, moving your chair closer to the client unnaturally, or other acts of forced warmth. In all cases, stylized behavior implies faked feeling, patterned closeness, too much attention to the maintenance of a smooth situation. The price of style is an inauthentic encounter.

Technique May Be Imperfect

It's impossible to isolate the best of all possible reactions so as to insure complete and perfect efforts. The crusade for perfection runs counter to humanness in the relationship, often causing the counselor to seek the "right technique" over concentration on the client's presence. Authentic human interaction may at times be awkward since there is often awkwardness in the attempt to experience another person deeply. Existing behavior constellations may just not fit. The words may be hard to find; the smooth ready response cannot do justice to the present event. At these times, why mandate perfection? Just appreciate what is happening and participate in it.

Technique Has Structure

The encounter operates within real limits. It has form. The interaction is partially determined by time, space, entry motives, expectations.

Shertzer and Stone agree and say:

> The working arrangement for conducting the relationship begins when the helper and the person to be helped come together. Invariably, the latter initially conceives the former as an authority or expert who is to take the lead, while his own role is usually preconceived as that of an "assistant." Both participants introduce their total life experiences into the relationship. Their attitudes stem from these experiences and determine how they relate to each other. The helper is expected to and often does give explanation or definition (sometimes tentatively and ambiguously) as to what may happen in the relationship and either or both are instrumental in establishing expected outcomes. The clues and cues each receives from the other determine ways of working together. Although varying amounts of freedom are given to the person who is to be helped, he must have an opportunity to respond and be expansive. Structure varies, depending upon the type of helping relationship, but its essential features — patterns of

stimuli and response — are always present. Structure enables the relationship to eventuate in growth and productivity. In reality, responsibility for the structure is reciprocal. Both the helper and the person to be helped have needs — to achieve, to be recognized, to be adequate — that determine structure and set in motion responses which the helping person must be prepared to meet if he is to build a helping relationship.* [Shertzer and Stone, 1974, p. 9]

Brammer and Shostrom (1968, pp. 204–205) add that structure provides the client with a frame, an orientation, a map, a dossier of his responsibilities so he knows where he is, who the counselor is, and why he is there. They refer to an analogy used by May to further make their point. Each person is traveling through life as though he were in a boat moving down a river. Without the structure of the river bank the water would flow in all directions. The banks of the river provide the limiting factors (the structure) which guide the boat and give it added power to go down stream. The individual is free to make his own choices, but always there seems to be a frame of reference which gives direction to the choice process. The client is thus aware of a plan of counseling.

Malcolm's Paradigm: Expanded

Thus far it has been stated that relating is not enough, that existential counselors do indeed use technique. Further, a series of assertions and definitions have been set forth that will help counselors better comprehend how they may use their technique in more existential and humanistic ways. Still, we have not fully addressed ourselves to the issue Patterson raised: What about existentialism and technique?

This section will present a model in which six technical areas are presented and explained, focusing among other things on the encounter and the client's environment, on both the interpersonal relationship and certain humanistic environmental processes, on the theoretical and practical, on ways of doing existential counseling and therapy.

It was said earlier that this monograph would just not replow old ground, but would give the practicing counselor and personnel worker some means of conceptualizing existential philosophy and practice in his day-to-day situation. That's our charge, especially in this section.

Malcolm (1968) set forth a model for viewing the techniques counselors-in-training need to move them from beginning status to the more effective and mature status of the trained professional.

* Reprinted from *Fundamentals of Counseling*, 2nd ed., by Bruce Shertzer and Shelley C. Stone © 1974 by Houghton Mifflin Company.

Malcolm, rightly so, focused his analysis on interpersonal or relationship techniques, not on behaviors needed to work for organizational change. We have expanded Malcolm's paradigm to include the environmental domain. The pinwheel-like cylinder in Figure 3, perhaps, more clearly describes Malcolm's idea and the authors' embellishments. The model has two major dimensions: 1) the person/person, and 2) the person/environment. The person/person dimension has three processes: 1) introgression, 2) intervention, and 3) implementation. The person/environment has three processes also: 1) research, 2) consultation, and 3) organization and development. Finally, each dimension and process operates on both a theory level (macroscopic) and a practice level (microscopic).

Before these ideas are expanded more fully, it is important to

FIGURE 3

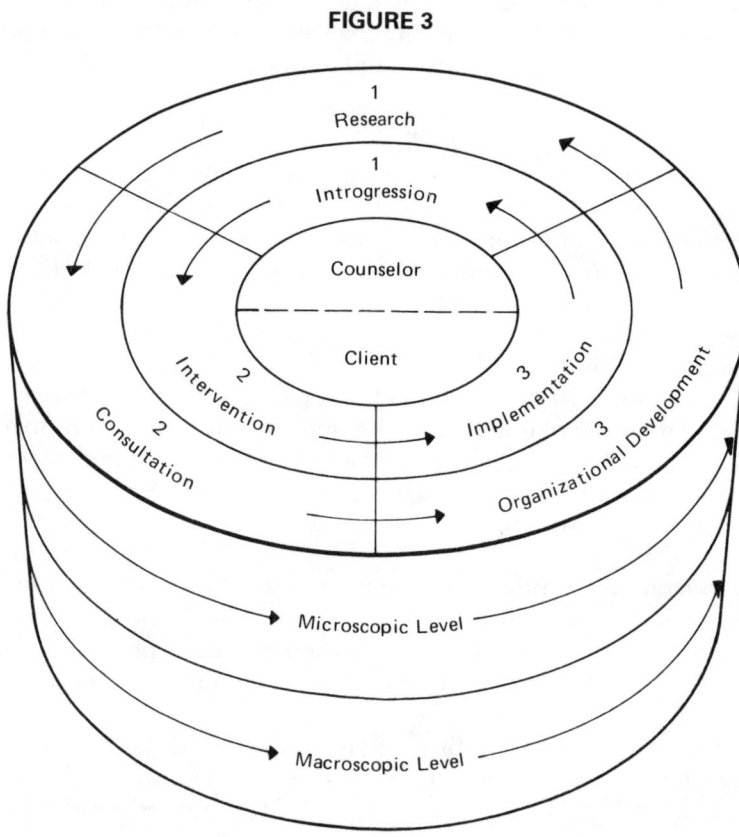

note that each dimension, each process, each level can be used as a parameter to define and select appropriate techniques.

The heart of the model is based on two ideas. First, the human encounter is the center of all counseling. Second, growth enhancing environments nourish and support helpful and productive human encounters. These two dimensions are given in the drawing as the two major parallel circles moving around the client and counselor in a pinwheel fashion. The circles are parallel because they show how the counseling relationship is constantly in touch and influenced by the world, i.e., the school, the community, the family — the environmental domain.

The Person/Person Dimension

The process subgroups in this factor include introgression, intervention, and implementation. Introgression means getting into the client's life space — seeing the world through his eyes. This is the domain of rapport, contact, touching, empathy. It entails the art of "being together" in a direct psychological way. This is first on the pinwheel because without the ability to establish contact, nothing else is truly possible; the encounter is never born. Also, to go on without introgressing is foolhardy since the counselor doesn't really know where to go; he and the client are forced to travel separate paths.

Intervention involves the process of selecting a method or plan of helping. Intervention planning is conscious, cognitive; it involves selecting the "best" counseling strategy. Intervention plans are answers to questions such as, "What can we do to solve this concern?" To do this effectively, counselors need to understand the process of helping clients become actively involved in framing action plans, in providing data for the planning, and must have a thorough knowledge of alternative means for arriving at answers to questions. This process is second, after introgression, because we can only develop plans after we know the needs and the world of the person with whom we are working.

Implementation means "follow through." This process makes or breaks counseling. Unless the plan is acted upon, nothing really changes. To have introgressed, to have designed a strategy, and then do nothing more is truly existential impotency. We are all too familiar with counselors who are able to establish rapport and may be expert at defining the dynamics in the life of the client, using the data to develop a grand strategy. Yet, they fall short when it comes to staying with the client during the movement from planning and understanding to action.

Thus, the person/person dimension leads from introgression through intervention to implementation. Malcolm elaborates:

> It should be noted that counselor behavior is characterized by a sort of pinwheel phenomenon. That is, when all three elements are present, introgression influences intervention which determines implementation which advances introgression which results in revised intervention, so on, in a continuous, interrelated process. According to my theory, this pinwheel phenomenon exists simultaneously at two levels whenever counseling is taking place.
>
> At the macroscopic level, it exists as the grand strategy of the overall process. It is to the macroscopic level that we have been referring hitherto in this paper. The contention here is that simultaneously at the microscopic level, it exists in every individual counselor response. On the microscopic level, every counselor response-verbal or nonverbal represents the implementation of an intervention that ideally was the consciously and cognitively determined result of the counselor's prior introgression.
>
> As a counselor educator helping the trainee with the process of becoming a counselor, I find the introgression/intervention/implementation pinwheel a useful conceptual tool for communication at the level of the individual counseling response as well as at the level of the overall process.*

The Person/Environment Dimension

We have been struck by the fact that so little attention has been devoted to training counselors to create "humane" environments. Psychological ecologists and community mental health personnel have turned our heads a bit, but we simply do not consider fully the client's environment or our own for that matter. Counselors are told that the relationship (direct service) is the core of their service, never fully arriving at the conclusion that relationships are best implemented in supportive, non-hostile, proactive, humane settings (Frey, 1971).

Too often a client's tentative change or growth is countered by the effects of a hostile environment that might have been positively altered had we taken the time.

The person/environment dimension has three sub-activities: research, consultation, and organizational development. In the broadest sense research means finding out about things. Our meaning of research is broad and includes any technique or strategy that may produce knowledge about the client and his world. Research, defined this way, is more inclusive than empirical science or ex-

* From "On Becoming a Counselor" by David D. Malcolm in *The Personnel and Guidance Journal*, 1968, 46:4, pp. 673–684. Copyright 1968 American Personnel and Guidance Association. Reprinted with permission.

perimental design or statistics. Researching, for us, includes learning about the client population, the culture, the sounds, the smells, the taste of the neighborhood. It may entail doing case studies, visiting homes, reading journal articles, talking, thinking and dreaming, and of course doing experiments. Research falls outside the person/person dimension because the action can occur without the client; it is extra-interview, extra-relationship activity. Still, researching produces knowledge and attitudes that directly influence the encounter.

The second person/environment element is consultation. Consultation is defined by Caplan (1964) as being "an interaction between professional persons — the consultant, who is the specialist, and the consultee, who evokes his help in regard to a current work problem with which he is having some difficulty and which he had decided is within the consultant's area of competence." To use Caplan's term, consultees for school counselors, for example, include the client's peers, his parents, his teachers, the principal, other pupil personnel workers, and others.

The times do not support the "school shrink" model, as a teacher termed it — sitting in an office seeing one client after another with little concern for outside issues. Involvement in institutions employing counselors means positive and helpful interactions with those in the client's world who can help (Dinkmeyer, 1968; Faust, 1968). Moreover, many general issues regarding the overall institutional environmental impact can first develop through consultation relationships, i.e., developing a more personal curriculum, closer contact with parents, improved communication with the community.

Banikiotes (1973) notes that most counselors are not prepared in their training programs to assume the consultant role; it's natural then that many are fearful of this involvement, retreating to the security of their office and their clients. Still the point remains, when overall effectiveness is considered the counselor must strive to maintain his encounters within the existing sociological matrix, employing the environment for the client's benefit whenever possible.

Consulting, as we define it, is not antithetical to the encounter nor tainted by the negativism of "social engineering" (Patterson, 1969). The relationship with others in the client's life begins with the client's needs and his permission, if necessary.

Consulting should develop out of, and alongside, the human relationship; to support it, nourish it, expand it. This kind of involvement in consultation has to include the client as part of the process.

The organizational element involves functions used in planning, altering, and administering programs; including the knowledge and skills necessary to influence others to move in mutually beneficial directions. This means knowing about power. May (1971) said that there is little satisfaction to be found in fleeing from legitimate power; impotency, powerlessness, and innocence (the lack of power realities) only lead to hostility and violence. Conversely, knowledge of the legitimate use of power can lead to beneficial growth and change. Power is real. Power is what change is about. Without it we can't change ourselves, others, or an institution.[1]

Stubbins (1970) notes that different counselors handle power in different ways: one group quickly accepts the institutional norm (their power is the institution), another denies power (they retreat from the decision-making process), while the best counselors are acutely aware of the power structure, seeking to be heard in places where decisions are made influencing the lives of their clients.

In summary, the person/environment dimension stresses that the counselor become involved in creating an environment that maximizes the human relationship, helping persons meet with each other in facilitative ways, and supporting the human or non-bureaucratic aspects of institutions. The generation of supportive institutions necessarily involves research, consultation, and organizational development techniques.

The Compatibility of Personal and Organizational Change

There is a current tendency to dichotomize the counselors' role into personal relationship functions and social engineering functions, casting the former into good light and the latter into bad. The message is to "not dirty yourself" with organizational development tasks. The argument continues to state that to be successful in one means to fail in the other. Success in consultation or research or organizational development necessarily negates interpersonal effectiveness (Patterson, 1968).

For the authors, the dichotomized position is neither accurate nor defensible for at least three reasons: external press, internal qualities, and narrow philosophy.

---

[1] Many have discussed organization change and power. Among the more useful discussions are given by Boyatzis (1969), Blake and Moulton (1961), Bennis (1966), and Bennis, Benne, and Chin (1969). Others have focused on how curricula and programs can be developed within institutions for personal development (Alschuler, 1969; Mogar, 1969; Ivey and Weinstein, 1970; Mosher and Sprinthall, 1970; Gibb, 1968, 1969, 1970).

External Press

Counseling, unlike medicine or law, is almost totally an institutionalized profession. Counselors are staff members in schools, hospitals, prisons, colleges, universities and agencies. They work for, and are part of, the larger social unit. Entry and participation in the institution is necessary for full functioning and for survival.

In schools, for example, other professional groups, i.e., teachers and administrators, have been active in asking counselors to become more involved in the institution's missions, suggesting that the counselor become more actively involved in curriculum development, out-reach programs, parent liaison work and so on. They see counselors as educators ("Aren't we all educators? — we work in a school."), and expect counselors to be responsive to institutional pressures (Kehas, 1970). With smaller budgets and increased social pressures and problems such as violence and drug abuse, staffs are unwilling to support a service that they perceive as outside the thrust of the school's major mission.

Also, existence outside the ongoing processes of institutions eventually will render the counselor professionally impotent; he has no power base nor support to continue his efforts.

Internal Qualities

Dichotomies force us to look at persons as males or females, as open or closed, soft or hard, weak or powerful, one or zero. It's just not that simple. At any one time, we may be male or female, open to this but not to that, receptive to Gene and not to Judy, afraid of academic failure but exhibit power in interpersonal relationships. Persons can attend a meeting, for example, on how to better design the new student union, deal effectively with the building committee, and later exhibit care, warmth, and openness in a therapeutic setting. These qualities are not antithetical, but demonstrate the varied and expansive traits that can exist simultaneously and comfortably within most persons.

Narrow Philosophy

Maslow, in his book *Eupsychian Management* (1965), noted how enlightened management methods at a company called Non-Linear Systems first captured his interest by validating his theory of human needs and also by violating his stereotype of businessmen; they shouldn't have been interested in human growth, but they were.

As we noted above, we are often caught on the horns of the

dilemma we construct in forming contradictive dichotomies, i.e., businessmen are less sensitive to human needs than counselors and psychologists, good persons care for people and bad persons care for organizations. If I accept X, then Y is not acceptable.

Two psychologists have thought about the resolution of apparent contradictions, Chenault (1966) and Shaw (Jourard and Overlade, 1966). Chenault says we need not select one alternative to the exclusion of the other. Countering the Aristotelian proposition that a belief in X contradicts a belief in Y, she presents an alternate philosophic model supporting a broader valuing of the totality of life. The philosophy is syntony. Essentially syntony involves the isolation of broader perspectives and the acceptance of natural contradictions. She says:

> A person may see, for example, cognition and conation as inseparable and falsely dichotomized concepts (synergy); he may see work and play as different, unique concepts, but existing simultaneously (compatible simultaneously); he may see frivolous and serious as different concepts which do not exist simultaneously but which can exist compatibly in a person at different times and to different degrees (compatible differentiation); or he may see polarities as combinations of the above possibilities. [Chenault, 1966]

Shaw takes this a step further by saying that the reconciliation of contradictions is a natural feature of the human organism's adaptation to himself and the world. Man seeks the stimulation of contradictions and receives satisfaction from finding larger perspectives that reconcile the apparent contradictions. The basic direction of persons is forward, becoming more inclusive at each step of growth. Perhaps his statement written sometime ago provides us with a view of a more inclusive frame for counselor role and technique based on man's personal enlargement potential.*

> A dawning construction of man as a self-expressive entity emerges in 1955 which prompts the prediction, stated earlier, that the counselor of the future will be viewed in different perspective than the counselor of the present. Sanford's concept of creative health summons a vision of man's realization of personal resources which is strengthened by Kelly's view of man's conceptual freedom and Murphy's view of man's capacity for enrichment through participation in his life milieu. Super's stress on building on the individual's assets and Foley's reference to circumventing implications of weakness or personal imbalance would seem to reflect something more than iso-

---

* Reprinted, with permission, from "Counseling," *Annual Review of Psychology*, Vol. 8, p. 373. Copyright © 1957 by Annual Reviews Inc. All rights reserved.

lated instances of positive perspectives. If so, society's perception of the counselor's role, as well as his own perception of it, may be shifting toward a broader interpretation of his function as a "human-resources consultant." As such, his interest in self-expressive styles of living might be expected to encompass a somewhat more limited kind of interest in pathology and rehabilitation as well as vocational and education choice. The brand of knowledge sought might at the same time be expected to revolve increasingly around the question of the nature of creative health, a question emerging, it would seem, from the construction of man as a self-expressive entity. [Shaw, 1957]

Summary

Indeed there is more to existential counseling than just relating. However, because existentialists have chosen to focus on certain philosophical themes, technical questions have not been fully articulated. The purpose of this chapter was to create a structure within which existential techniques can be developed.

First technique was defined: asserting that it should be based on client need, that understanding is prior to action, that technique should be flexible, that it can't stand alone, that it is often best defined after the fact, that good technique is not stylized, that it may be imperfect, and that it has structure.

Second, Malcolm's paradigm was expanded to include two dimensions for viewing technical roles and functions: the person/person dimension (including introgression, intervention, implementation), the person/environment dimension (including research, consultation, organizational development).

Finally, the point was made that it is possible for counselors to work comfortably and effectively in both the interpersonal and institutional domain. One does not cancel the other.

6

Person Centered Assessment

Assessment in Counseling

Counseling inevitably involves the collection of data. Data are important at all levels and for all functions. In moving closer through introgression, certainly in planning intervention, and in implementation, data are vital to the processes of consultation and development.

Few question the fact that counselors constantly seek out data and incorporate the material into their work with clients. However, many differ as to the assessment model that should be used. Some counselors rely primarily on objective, standardized instruments to help them collect, synthesize, and organize data. Others prefer a more subjective, observational method, i.e., "looking at" clients and using their own standards as a base for making assessment statements. The test user believes that his approach, based on item selection, validation, and external norming, insures assessment accuracy. He thinks these data are relatively uncontaminated by his values, his biases, his prejudices. The data are objective, clean, and so it is thought more true. The other type of counselor trusts his own experience; his values and biases have a legitimate place in the data collection since he holds that all data must be validated within himself.

Standardized tests tell us how we are like others — the data are said to be nomothetic. The clinical method centers on one person, the interconnections of qualities within an individual — the data are termed idiographic.

We are not interested in pitting test users against observers; nor are we interested in raising historical arguments between the "scientist" and the "artist," between the "hard" and "soft" therapist. First of all it's a silly fight, and secondly these are just not the times for rabble rousing. Meehl (1956) concluded some time ago that both approaches have real merit, that each accounts for different aspects of human variance, and that each can serve the other since a combination of both approaches appears to have the greatest potential for improving assessment practice.

Certainly there is a great need to improve assessment practices. All of us have heard about or may have seen persons who have been hurt by faulty assessment. All know stories that go: "My high school counselor told me to take the general program. I'm glad I didn't because I may not have gotten my Ph.D.;" "Our son was put in a special class. They just told us, we weren't asked. Does he really belong there?" Regardless of their validity, the impact of statements such as these raise questions in the minds of persons about the use of assessment procedures in counseling and education.

Today the counselor's clientele is becoming more vocal in their criticism of the potential abuses in assessment. They are asking among other things that counselors become more responsible and accountable for their assessment decisions, and that something be done to humanize assessment practices.

Hopefully, this chapter may help counselors face the challenge regarding the use of assessment data in counseling. First, we will develop a model to insure that the widest array of data is collected and used, and secondly speculate about how data might be used more openly.

Parameters for Data Collection

Most existential counselors and theorists advocate using data for making diagnoses. Surely part of this emphasis stems from the fact that many existential therapists were trained in medical schools, often receiving advanced work in psychoanalysis. Still, part of the interest in data stems from being drawn to facts about the lives of persons. Existentialists are person centered; they enjoy knowing the past, the places, the present, the names, the dreams, the things about people. They relish knowing about the lives of persons.

Earlier we said that the encounter between the counselor and client is complex. Counselors are given a bewildering mass of data; verbal reports, non-verbal behavior, observed and uttered in what seems to be the most complex drama. Chronological order is often not important and themes can change instantly in the drama. Without some reference points, conceptual maps, or data collection frameworks, the data are difficult to identify, to sort, to understand, to articulate.

Our model uses three data collection parameters to help order the drama: the philosophic parameter, the experiential parameter, and the technical parameter. Each parameter encompasses nomothetic (test) and idiographic (observational) data.

The Philosophic Parameter

The philosophic parameter focuses on the client's assumptions about life. What does he believe? What does he value? What does he accept as true? Our assumptions are important because assumptions allow or disallow action; they set limits on our behavior. If we believe the world is disordered, we are less likely to seek order. A child who believes that arithmetic is too difficult, will act accordingly. A student who believes he has a right to the facts, will often actively seek out the facts.

We define philosophy in this instance in a rather special way. The philosophic parameter does not necessarily tap metaphysics, epistemology, theology, and so on. Our meaning is more person centered — what is the person's philosophy? It doesn't have to be philosophical in the academic meaning of the term. It is a philosophy-in-the-person. Some might call this the person's "philosophy of life."

Sometime ago one of the authors met with a young man enrolled in an undergraduate engineering program at a large Midwestern university. The client said he was unhappy with his academic progress since he was consistently earning marginal grades in spite of the fact that he was spending more time than others in his studies. His studies took almost all of his time and energy. "I'm on a treadmill with no pay-off," he said. During the second or third session he began to explore his values, stating he believed in the saying "where there's a will there's a way." He said that hard work and effort alone could conquer all foes. He used the saying to justify his efforts in study. Moreover, he didn't question the assumption. It was a fact and needed no further scrutiny. This is a good example of what we mean by data from the philosophic parameter. This young man lived on the basis of the assumption that hard work conquers all.

Some other statements we have heard include: "I'm a born loser," "I just can't control my reactions," "We're all pawns of fate," "Look on the sunny side," "What's the use?"

Philosophy-in-the-person is not abstract; it's rooted in action; it's not neutral. Philosophy carries it's logical consequences, action based on assumption (Denney and Sydow, 1973). Counselors, therefore, need to observe and listen carefully because philosophic statements need not sound at all like academic philosophy. Rather concrete, ordinary statements often have profound philosophical meaning for clients. Sometimes, in fact, theoretical and overly abstract bull sessions about philosophy are not nearly as productive in tapping this area as talks about how the clients live their everyday life. What are the assumptions they make in doing the routine tasks in their present life?

Ellis (1962) and Kelly (1955) are two theorists who speak directly to the point of philosophy-in-the-person. For example, Ellis believes that, for all practical purposes, the phrases and sentences we keep telling ourselves are, or become, our thoughts and emotions. Ellis thinks that neurotic and self-defeating behavior is the result of poor, irrational or illogical thought or a faulty philosophy of life. Kelly takes a more phenomenological position than Ellis, stating that all persons organize their world through forms, patterns, or constructs; each construct system psychologically channeling the person's perception of the world and eventually altering behavior.

The Experiential Parameter

The second data collection parameter covers the person's experience; it centers on how the client participates in life outside the boundary of the interview. The data include habitual patterns of interaction with the physical environment *(umwelt)*, with interpersonal relationships *(mitwelt)*, and with self *(eigenwelt)*. Other data may include occupational and educational history, medical history, hobbies and leisure activities, sexual activity, and so on. The intent of the experiential parameter is to grasp as fully as possible the person's life and life history.

In gathering these data, both past and present data are sought. Clients do not strip away their past when they enter counseling. Further the interaction in counseling, and with others, is a product of the interface between personality factors and concrete situations. Persons and their environment inevitably affect each other. We want to know about this. It is important to know something about the person's family, his school record and habits, his medical disabilities, his home town, his cultural and racial identity. Hopefully, the collection of life experience data will increase the counselor's perspective; his ability to see patterns, themes, central dimensions in the life of the client; his having a sense of the relative importance of one event in the field of all events as they influence the client. Too often, counselors lose this sense of over-all perspective.

For example, one of our clients, the young wife of a graduate student, entered counseling because of fatigue, tenseness, irritability. Taken at face value and without other data her symptoms might have led the counselor to focus on her as the "problem." "She can't cope," "has unexpressed anger," the counselor might say. But complete data revealed that she is the mother of two children under four, she lives in a small three room apartment, doesn't have a car or washing machine (diapers are a real hassle), needs some dental work, has gained twenty pounds since she was married, and her husband is facing the pressure of preliminary exams for his degree. With the added data her complaints seem more natural, not pathological symptoms at all. Furthermore, the counselor and the client now have a broader base to work from in planning intervention strategies, i.e., a woman's group, referral to financial aids, a phone call to the housing office, contact with the student health facility, and, of course, individual counseling.

Idiographic case study methods have been especially fruitful in providing experiential data. The method involves assuming a longitudinal frame of reference within the life of one person; it is an intensive data gathering technique for working within the life space of a person. Such studies may be called $N = 1$, life history analysis, individual case study, case reports, and so on. A number of theorists have provided us with rationales and procedures for making our $N = 1$ research more valid, reliable, and more potent clinically. They include: Buhler's (1971) and Buhler and Massarik's (1968) work on life histories; Allport's (1965) structural analysis technique for personal documents; Dailey's (1971) programmed cases; Kelly's (1955) repertory grid; Swensen's (1968) method for case conceptualization.

Others have given us models for organizing life history data. Blocher and Shaffer (1971) distinguish between chronological and hierarchial models for the analysis of experience. Chronological models include Erikson's (1963) eight stages of man, Super's (1957) occupational development stages, and Buhler's (1933) life cycle periods. The hierarchical model is best represented by Maslow's (1959) steps toward self-actualization.

TABLE 1
The Gilmore System — Developmental Stages

	Infancy and Childhood	Adolescence	Early Adulthood	Middle Age	Old Age
Work	Explore and manipulate the world	Helping at home	First job and/or continued education	Possible job change	Retirement
	Acquire language and concepts	Coping with school work	Continued vocational planning	Re-enter school	Alternatives to remunerated activity
		Vocational exploration		Redefining vocational aspirations	Coping with real and arbitrary limits
				Prepare for retirement	
Interpersonal Relations	Approach others	Reciprocity or "taking role of the others"	Marriage and family	Break-up of family with loss of children	"Generation gap"
	Allow others to approach	Sharing outside family group	Friendship	Changing roles in marriage	Sharing the wisdom of experience
	Differentiate family and friends, strangers	Sexual identity	Co-workers	Importance of friends and co-workers	Coping with loneliness
		Cooperation and competition	Community relations		
Aloneness	Allow "mothering one" out of sight	Uniqueness and accountability of self	Ability to maintain oneself and help care for others	Loss of parents	Facing one's own death
	Stand and walk alone	Relationship to higher order of meaning (Religion, Humanity, etc.)	Tolerate being misunderstood	Meaning of physical suffering and death	Loss of spouse
	Separate sense of "Me-ness"		Carve out personal philosophy of life	Continued integration of philosophy of life	Loss of friends
	Self-initiated play				

Leona E. Tyler, *The Work of the Counselor* © 1969. Reprinted by permission of Prentice-Hall, Inc., Englewood Cliffs, New Jersey.

Gilmore (Tyler, 1969, p. 23) combined the chronological approach with personal involvement (see Table 1) to yield a two-way grid for organizing experiential data around developmental expectations at given points in life. Blocher and Shaffer (1971) also make the distinction between life stage, life space, and life style. Life stage conceptualizations focus on the client's place in chronological and cultural time, i.e. the onset of puberty, graduation, retirement, grade in school, specifying the cultural and social expectations set forth for the client. Life space conceptualizations consider physical environment, i.e., ghetto or rural, rich or poor. Life style is more value based; it centers on the client's general and characteristic approach to life based on his philosophy.

The Technical Parameter

The technical parameter concentrates on the client's behavior in the interview, it focuses on the client's techniques. As we said in the preceding chapter, the client's technique is what shows — how the client acts and reacts. It is what we would see on a videotape or hear on a recording.

A number of classification systems have been developed to describe client technique. The most common systems are the diagnostic nosologies used in medical and psychiatric practice. Lately, however, the use of such nosologies and their symptom categories such as manic-depressive, paranoid, and so on have been strongly criticized since the reliability of the assigned diagnostic labels doesn't always hold. (It is not at all uncommon to get four different diagnoses for the same observable behavior from four professionals.)

Others have organized client technique in different ways. Back (1962) analyzes language according to two dimensions or themes. One dimension assesses the degree of immediacy in the client's communication, ranging from a "signal" impinging directly on a particular person to a more rigid symbolism that can only be understood via a code. The second dimension relies on the fundamental orientation of the individual, either cognition or encounter. Encounter talk is personal, cognitive talk is abstract and universal. Therefore, Back's model gives us a direct/cognition cell (the perception of an object and its objective description), a cognition/symbolic cell (machine language, talking in Fortran), an encounter/symbolic cell (a university lecture), and finally an encounter/direct cell (I-thou language, poetry, lover's chatter).

In the first chapter a method for analyzing the interrelationship among therapy approaches was presented (Frey, 1972; Rosso and

Frey, 1973). This paradigm can also be used to analyze client technique since the two axes, goals and processes, also describe what clients do in counseling; "This is what I'm doing and why." Type one (cell one) clients employ rational processes toward insight goals, type two (cell two) use affective process for insight, type three (cell three) employ affective processes for action goals, and type four (cell four) use rational processes for action.

Kagan and others at Michigan State University (Kagan, Krathwohl, and Farguhar, 1965) studied nonverbal technique, developing a typology of nonverbal behavior. Among the major components of their typology are: the sources of the nonverbal behavior, the degree of client awareness, and the duration of the behavior.

In brief summary, the technical parameter concentrates on gathering data about the client's technique, what he says and what he does in the interview. Models developed by Back, Frey, and Kagan are given as examples of systems that may help the counselor to order technical data.

Epistemological Components of Assessment Practice

Thus far person centered assessment involves the use of both idiographic and nomothetic data gathered across three parameters: the philosophic, the experiential, the technical. How do we use these data? How do we combine this fact with that? What is our theory of data?

These are questions of epistemology or the study of knowing. Epistemology examines the rules by which a person can come to the conclusion "I know." Kohlberg and Mayer (1972) analyzed three streams of educational theory and the epistemological base of each theory. Their analysis holds merit because their three ideologies, psychological theories and epistemologies, can be used to describe three styles of viewing data for assessment, three ways to arrive at knowledge.

Counselors who rely primarily on standardized instruments are most like educators who accept a cultural transmission ideology and epistemologies emphasizing knowledge as that which is objective and repetitive, that which is based on sense experience, and that which can be measured, tested, and promulgated. Their world view stresses a potent environment acting upon a less potent learner. Interest is shown in external states and conditions, that which is seen directly. *The data are outside the skin.*

B. F. Skinner (1971) is perhaps the most representative of persons holding these views. He says:

> We can follow the path taken by physics and biology by turning directly to the relation between behavior and the environment and neglecting . . . states of mind . . . We do not need to discover what personalities, states of mind, feelings . . . intentions . . . or other prerequisites of autonomous man are in order to get on with a scientific analysis of behavior. [Skinner, 1971, p. 15]

In direct contrast to Skinner's position, others stress a more romantic point of view founded on the ideas of Rousseau and other educational romantics. Learning is a natural "flowering," a simple unfolding of natural positive capacities. Knowledge is established on an immediate inner awareness and experience of self. Truth is self-awareness, insight, inner self-knowledge on both the emotional and cognitive planes. These assessors believe those who ignore inner states in the name of "science" do so at their peril, since the real data are within the person himself. For them, *the data are inside the skin.*

A third position integrates data from external and internal states into a functional epistemology. Kohlberg and Mayer call this the cognitive-developmental view. This doctrine draws heavily on the educational philosophies of Dewey and the developmental psychology of Piaget. Persons are to be understood through interaction with the environment since internal structures are produced by two invariant processes: accommodation (adaptive change to outer circumstances), and assimilation (incorporation of the external into the inner organization with transfer to new circumstances) (Hunt, 1960, p. 356). The cognitive-developmental view

> . . . takes inner experience seriously by attempting to observe thought process rather than language behavior and by observing valuing processes rather than reinforced behavior. In doing so, however, it combines interviews, behavioral tests, and naturalistic observation methods in mental assessment. The cognitive-developmental approach stresses the need to examine mental competence or mental structure as opposed to examining only performance, but it employs a functional rather than an introspective approach to the observation of mental structure. [Kohlberg and Mayer, 1972, p. 461]

In short, the cognitive-developmental approach does not focus on inner experience or on external behavior by epistemological fiat, but strives to integrate and coordinate both through a systematic procedure. To return to our analogy, both *inside the skin* and *outside the skin* data are valued, are collected, and are analyzed.

The Principle of Two-Headed Validation

Each assessment situation holds, at least, two persons, each having *inside the skin* and *outside the skin* data. As the counselor, for example, gathers data he becomes actively involved in certain actual processes (scores tests, sits to think quietly about the case) and with inner experiences caused by the data he gets from the client (builds internal models to explain what has occurred).

Too often the other person in the dyad doesn't know what the external behavior means and is not given access to the model building process. The process of building these models in assessment situations is essentially a process of construct validation (Frey, 1973). In the process of developing an explanation and description of the data the counselor mentally forms clusters of data; linking the clusters, whenever possible into a hierarchical network of interlocking clusters. The counselor makes sense out of his data clusters by finding more general and abstract constructs that define the data more parsimoniously. Data are gathered, ordered, investigated, validated with personal theoretical bias, and descriptive and explanatory principles are established. The final steps involve the articulation of statements and hypotheses; finally, testing the hypotheses in the real world. The network of data, abstractions, and constructs yields a conceptual model of the person or phenomena under study (Cronbach and Meehl, 1955). To go one step further, the counselor in his construct validation attempts to build an internal model that is just like the person he is assessing.

The principle of two-headed validation states that the model building process can't be singular if the model is to have validity. Unless such models face the real tests — what does someone else think about this? — we can never be certain as to their truth.

Assessment is a two person process, involving constant feedback, openness to new data, and new interpretation. Not only is the final assessment statement or hypothesis up for review, the process of hypotheses generation is also public. Kelly offers this observation about two-headed validation.

> Since the model of man in humanistic research is the experimenter rather than the subject, it follows that the humanistic psychologist will make the most of what those whom he has enlisted to help him have to say. Too often, it turns out that the experiment the psychologist thinks he is performing is not the one in which his subject is engaged. If the two experimenters are to collaborate each needs some idea of what the other is doing... at the very least humanistic research means that each

person who participates should at some point be apprised of what the "experimenter" thinks he is doing and what is considered evidence of what. It is of equal importance to ask what the "subject" thinks is being done, and what he considers evidence of what. [Kelly, 1969, p. 136]

Tyler believes the process of sharing data between counselor and client is a function of a more hopeful movement in applied psychology that uses consultation rather than professional elitism, subject participation in research design, and client interpretation of test data as foundational precepts. The general point is this: "Any project on which I am engaged as a human psychologist is not *my* project but *our* project" (Tyler, 1973, p. 1024).

The Live Case Study: A Prototype

It is a natural question to ask how person-centered assessment might differ from traditional methods. Perhaps the most glaring difference is that the client's ground and position are as valid as the assessor's; the cardinal postulate states that "it's the client's data and life, not the counselor's."

Further, all data are seen as important, useful, and valuable. Data orthodoxy or stylish affectations are seen as just that — close-minded pedantry. If the situation necessitates careful study of the client's budget then these are important data. If a standardized instrument is needed and useful, use it. If not, don't use it but collect the data that will help the client move through to the resolution of the issue in question. As was said before, the data used in such cases are idiographic and nomothetic, personal and societal, empirical and phenomenological.

Person-centered assessment is also marked by the fact that the data inference process is open to "public" review. This means that the client should not only participate in the data generation process and have access to the results, it also means that he should have access to the way data are handled, the inner clinical process itself. Counselors should be able to answer the question, "How did you arrive at that conclusion?"

We have been tinkering with a way to facilitate this kind of open system assessment (Frey and Conyne, 1972). This tinkering with the ideas led to the development of the "life case study." At this point in time the method has only been applied to persons enrolled in counselor education programs, to help them better understand the process of assessment and also to receive feedback about themselves as assessors. However, we offer the "live case" as a prototype of newer ways to use data in counseling and for making personnel decisions of one kind or other. Certainly, the model is incomplete, but it is offered in the spirit of a heuristic and tentative hypothesis.

The "live case" involves both the client and several assessors in a structured group process directed toward data collection, synthesis, analysis, and validation. The assessors (could be counselors, teachers, school administrators, for example) divide themselves into three groups of equal size. After selecting from among the three data collection parameters previously mentioned, each group elects a group spokesman or interview leader; however, each member is free to ask questions. During a caucus period the small group develops an assessment plan, and considers case history and test data, if it is available.

The client is briefed about the purpose and philosophy of the method and is told he can refuse to answer any query and that he can expect to have both strong emotional and cognitive reactions to the process. He is also asked if he believes in the usefulness of self-disclosure and the potential utility of the method. No client should, of course, participate in this unless he understands the process and is committed to it.

Each of the three groups meets separately with the client, one group focusing on philosophy, another on experience, and a third on the here-and-now technique.

The groups caucus again and develop a set of simple declarative sentences they believe to be true for the client. Statements that cannot get consensus support are not entered. If a specific decision is to be considered, i.e., vocational choice feedback, college choice, or interpersonal issues, each group makes a recommendation about the decision in question.

The three groups, the client, and a process manager reconvene as a total community. Each group writes its sentences on a blackboard and presents their ideas verbally to the total community. At this point, the client is encouraged to give feedback and to evaluate the group's statements, considering the process of data collection and analysis as well as the content. Group members are also urged to contribute. In all instances in which the method was used the dialogue has been open, human, and lively, with sentences being revised, added to, rejected and new hypotheses generated.

Throughout the process, enthusiasm and the level of participation remain high. For many, both clients and assessors, it is an intense emotional and cognitive experience. Reactions from all groups confirmed the authors' expectations that the assessors would respond in a constructive and sensitive manner. For the client and assessor the live case method provides high levels of growth-inducing, sensing, sharing, and self-validating data.

Summary

Counselors have recently been asked to deal effectively with abuses or alleged abuses in assessment practice; they have been asked among other things to become more responsible and accountable for their assessment decisions and to attempt to humanize assessment practices. In terms of this, this chapter presents a model that, hopefully, answers these queries.

First of all, counselors should strive to gather the widest array of data possible; from the person's beliefs and values (the philosophic parameter), from his life history (the experiential parameter), and from his behavior here and now (the technical parameter). Secondly, these data are best combined to yield accurate facts when both *inside the skin* and *outside the skin* data are sought and used.

Further, through the principle of two-headed validation, the counselor and client alike have total access to the assessment process and the conclusions drawn. Finally, the live case study method was presented as a tentative prototype of a more person-centered assessment method.

7

Will and Transition

Profile of Will

I said once to a boy, aged five, that he need not be afraid of a lion, for the lion would run away if only he would look him straight in the eyes. His next question was: "And a lamb can sometimes eat up a wolf, can't it." "You didn't believe my story about the lion," said I. "No, not really — ." [Ferenczi, 1950, p. 203]

All successful counseling reaches a point when the counselor's insight into the situation is not enough; this is the point when the client goes it alone, has to face the issue by himself. In Ferenczi's case, the little boy wasn't about to face lions with courage alone no matter how much Ferenczi was convinced that it was the child's fight and that he, the therapist, couldn't fight lions for him. These times are times when the client has to deal with will, his will, his power to act and change.

Early in the history of modern psychology the anatomy of will and will power was a common theme. William James, Franz Brentano and some of the founding fathers of existentialism grappled with the problem of how persons move through the resolution of life problems by reaching for the object to be reconciled with, and marshalling their resources to face the issue (Wilson, 1972; Barclay, 1971). However, Freud changed this thrust by stating that behavior is caused by the interaction of unconscious and conscious forces, often rendering acts of the will impotent. All we do, so it was said, is work out unconscious agenda of one type or other. The force of this idea transferred the attention of the professional community to the unconscious and irrational parts of the human personality while ignoring acts of the will.

Too, the popular Victorian idea that all one needed to do to be successful was to keep your nose to the grindstone, work hard, focus your forces and energy on the task at hand, proved to be a gross generalization. Freud's theories acted as a needed counterbalance to the unbridled will of such popular ideas as Horace Greeley's "go west young man" philosophy and Charles Sumner's "manifest destiny." Will was an important element in opening the frontier, for example, but surely not the only element. And Americans began to realize it.

The behavioristic learning theories also directed attention away from the analysis of the will, because their success was based on the premise that a person's behavior is set by the kinds of stimulus and contingencies he is or was exposed to. Will was hit from one side by the psychoanalysts and from the other by the behaviorists. It became unacceptable to talk about will; it was naive and smacked of some pre-scientific oversimplified ideas of personal maturation. "Persons can't really change themselves, the forces of the environment and the unconscious are too great," they said.

Still, all practicing counselors and therapists were vividly aware of the fact that unless the client somehow picked up the reins and took charge of the situation no real change was possible. Support without client action, insight without acting upon the knowledge, counselor understanding and client passivity, or reinforcement without implementation, all really render the therapy unsuccessful. At best it is only a rehearsal for a performance that will never be acted.

Wheelis says:

> Toward the end of the long analyses that now have become so common, the therapist may find himself wishing that the patient were capable of more push, more determination, a greater willingness to make the best of it. Often this wish eventuates in remarks to the patient: "People must help themselves;" "Nothing worthwhile is achieved without effort"; "You have to try." Such interventions are seldom included in case reports, for it is assumed that they possess neither the dignity nor effectiveness of interpretation. Often an

analyst feels uncomfortable about such appeals to volition, as though he were using something he didn't believe in, and as though this would have been unnecessary had only he analyzed more skillfully. The deficiency of will in the patient is mirrored by the loss, in the analyst, of a belief in the efficacy of will. The same culture produces both patient and analyst, and it is a culture in which the strength of individuals is no longer thought to be located in the strength of will. [Wheelis, 1958, pp. 42–43]

Still, will has survived, at least in the hearts of counselors. Recently, however, there has been a revived interest in the topic. Among some of the recent works that deal with will are: May's *Love and Will* (1969), Wheelis's *Quest for Identity* (1958) and *The Desert* (1969), Wilson's chapter on will in *New Pathways in Psychology: Maslow and the Post-Freudian Revolution* (1972), Frankl's *The Will to Meaning: Foundations and Application of Logo Therapy* (1969), and Assagioli's two books *The Training of the Will* (1966), and *The Act of Will* (1973).

These writers are saying that contemporary man is partly to blame for his current plight of alienation, loneliness, and meaninglessness by fault of his own self-definition. Persons who define themselves as pawns of fate (either by the unconscious or an engineered society) find it very difficult to see themselves actively involved in proactive movement. They find it difficult to take a firm stand and easy to modify themselves, to alter their values, to change their reactions, to avoid final decisions. The key words are flexibility, adjustment, reaction; not firmness, solidarity, and proaction.

Unless persons are able to say "I can" or "I will," little change is possible.

Potency

The counselor faces the issue of will at the transition point when the client needs to take the initiative in his own therapy. For example, a client resolves to "go to college," another "to seek employment actively." As May says (1969, p. 218) will is involved at that point when the client organizes himself so that *movement* in a certain direction or toward a certain goal may take place.

What is involved in facilitating these acts of the will? First the counselor must be strong enough to influence change in the client. Like it or not, counselors are in the change business (Frey, 1971). Some time ago, the authors were asked to identify what we thought was the single most important trait a counselor should have. We concluded it was potency. Potency entails being proactive, a person who builds, a person who is active, a person who will not hinder the client's development. Synonyms for potency are power, strength, effectiveness — traits not often assigned to counselors by clients or the general public. Potency is the foundation of change and clients come to us to change.

For us potency is before such qualities in counselors as caring, affection, acceptance, and sensitivity. If we care about, accept, and become sensitive to the client's life, but cannot help him through the relationship to work toward change, then we have failed. The caring is just so much fluff.

We know that potency can be good or bad. Certainly Hitler had power, but so did Pope John XXIII and Gandhi. And so do Rogers, Williamson, and Ellis; each is different yet potent in his own way. The effective counselor is able to become fully human in the encounter, to attend fully to the client's existence, yet maintain his strength to move through to resolution.

The potent counselor is not some sort of whirling dervish of power in the encounter. There is no call for random and unabashed application of power. Rather, we suggest that counselors have the strength to work for beneficial client change within the boundaries of a true existential encounter; further, they must have the good sense to understand how to apply their strength. More often than not, for example, counselor strength is needed as much for allowing the client to move forward on his own. Potency can involve restraint as well as action.

May (1969, p. 243) believes that power is potentiality and potentiality points toward the future, it is something that will happen. The act of will serves the counselor with a promissory note. He owes himself some future activity, in this case the helping of a client. He says "let it happen," "I will help this client," "I will do it."

Therefore, the first step the counselor takes in the change process is that of willing help. This may seem so basic, so elemental, yet without this statement of commitment little is really possible. The willing of helpfulness serves the change process by first validating the client's situation by saying, in effect, "I accept you and your circumstances and will deal with it." Moreover, the willingness to help usually intensifies the interaction, making it more centered, more personal, and more vital. Also, the counselor's will to help causes him to focus his energy and to organize his capacities so as to facilitate the movement to change. In short, the will to help serves as a sign of commitment to the client and as a rallying point for the counselor.

We are not saying that counselors can will change for clients. Yet, we believe that the act of intending change is primary, since without that act growth and change is inhibited. Clients typically enter counseling making "I can't" statements: "I can't choose between art and English," "I can't face my parents," "I can't seem to get it together." Just think how ridiculous and futile the whole counseling enterprise would be if the counselor, too, says, "I can't"; "I can't help you with that," "Don't expect me to commit myself to your problem." Potency entails being able to say "I can" and "I will" to the client.

Secondly, of course, potency entails being able to deliver, to follow through, to implement. Being able to help involves the six areas of technical skill discussed in chapter five (introgression, intervention, implementation, research, consultation, and organizational development). Moreover, it means existing in the state of "I am." The counselor is able to say "I can help you," "I will do it" and "here I am — let's get on with it." Saying "I am" forces the counselor's presence to the front, engaging the counselor and client in a wholehearted encounter. When this occurs, both counselor and client sense increased interpersonal awareness and a sense of movement and exhilaration. They confirm and validate each other in the relationship.

The Point of Transition

Valid and meaningful client change is seen in a changed life outside the encounter. The standard against which counseling is judged uses client-initiated action as the unit of measurement. That is, successful counseling leads to taking the process and products of counseling and applying them in the real world. Change occurring only in counseling relationship is of little value since the client is unable to integrate the counseling experience into a changing life.

For example, consider the client who because of the free existential atmosphere in counseling becomes more free with the counselor, talks openly about this and that, but remains constricted with his peers and parents. Also, consider the case where the client makes decisions quite easily in the counseling relationship yet cannot act on the decision in real life. In these cases there is no transfer, no transition, from being in-relationship to being-in-the-world. Figure 4 shows this graphically. Change, to become fully implemented and to have lasting beneficial effect, must move from the relationship to the world.

FIGURE 4

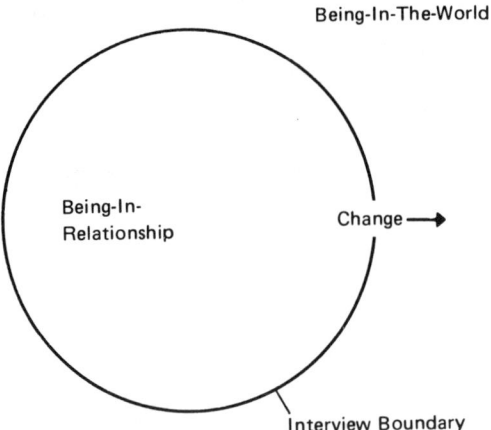

We are saying directly that counseling is not its own thing. Counseling is goal directed and the main goals are change and termination. We want the client to change, to grow, to further develop, so that counseling becomes unnecessary. In short, we want individuals to move through counseling to a point where they no longer need the counselor, but can trust and experience life on their own. Needless to say, there is often a great deal of pain at the point of transition. Sometimes it is the counselor who needs to keep the client as his client. At other times the client has to remain a client. In both cases they refuse to accept the pain of termination and the responsibility of change.

We have come to see counseling as a practice relationship having these qualities: 1) counseling carries the expectation for both parties that the relationship, as such, is temporary, 2) counseling is seen as a time to set aside, to review, to look ahead, to try on newer modes of experience and behavior, and 3) counseling provides an opportunity to make a concerted effort toward some goal. It is as if clients use the encounter as practice for real life.

When we take this view, then, how can we describe the encounter as real? Within counseling the mutuality, the depth of communication, the spontaneity, and feeling tone are real. These elements cannot be manufactured or simulated. In addition the client and counselor are real persons, performing real acts. However, in another sense counseling is less than fully real because of the structure; counseling as such is removed, taken out of, the ongoing life of the person.

This leads us to the point where the practice is transferred to the outside world, the point of transition. Rather than having the limited view of change within the encounter, this larger perspective forces us to view change in the total life of the client, inside the relationship, outside it, before it and after it.

What does the idea of the transition point hold for the client? First, the client gains a more sure sense of who he is in terms of the past, present, and future. He gains a more utilitarian sense of his own reality. But perhaps the major point for the client to consider is his own responsibility for action. Outside the encounter, "I have to do it. No one outside myself really has charge over my changes," he might say.

In accepting responsibility for action the client *drives* through to application. He takes an active stance toward the use of the counseling relationship for change. At this point the client moves toward life, the true reality. As Figure 4 shows, he drives through to being-in-the-world. The transition entails movement from being a client, to a potent client, to a potent person, or movement into counseling, through counseling, into the ongoing real world.

Indices of Transition

How does the counselor come to know that the client is moving toward transition? Of course, the simplest index is that the client terminates, but this can occur for defensive reasons as well as positive ones. Here are some of the phenomena the authors have observed as being signs that the client is moving away from the relationship toward the world.

Language

The client's language becomes clearer. The meaning is more open and less clouded and ambiguous. Further there are certain grammatical signs, among which is the increased use of declarative sentences. Whereas beginning clients talk in circles without strong emphasis and without the use of periods, the terminating clients often make more direct, simple statements punctuated by the period. The form of their language itself indicates the stand they are taking. It doesn't just taper off and fall away. These clients are more certain of their beliefs, values, and preferences and say so. Further, they have the ability to form their thoughts and express them simply and directly, punctuated by the crispness and sureness of the period.

Demands on the Counselor

Terminating clients often place demands on the counselor to validate their new attitudes and behavior. It might take the form of approving their new behavior, or acting as a safe and trial person with whom they can become intimate or whatever. In these cases, the clients begin to move from the self-centered motives that brought them to counseling. They begin to look around for another person to share their growth, to participate with them in their life outside the boundary of the therapeutic encounter. Counseling, itself, no longer meets the clients' needs and they begin to demand more.

Dissolution of the Technical Parameter

The structured behaviors of the client-counselor relationships no longer seem appropriate or make much sense. Rather than meet each week to talk about their life they want to live their life. The careful and often slow analysis of feeling and behavior often seems like a bore and a waste of time. They no longer want to do counseling-like things, but rather often become impatient with the process itself, feeling they can do this on their own.

At this point, the counselor and client often begin to experience the fact that the counseling relationship is more of a hindrance than a help. Moreover, there is less difference between how the client acts in counseling and how he acts in the world. The technical parameter within counseling mixes and merges with actual real-life behavior.

Real Feeling

Often there is a significant change in how the client perceives the counselor. Whereas, initially the counselor was often a remote professional, an all knowing person, who may have been very kind and effective, clients begin to see the counselor as "just another person" with weaknesses and strengths. The client's vision is more accurate, he doesn't need to have a counselor, he begins to focus on the human part of the counselor. If there is affection it's because the counselor and the client truly like each other; if there is anger, it's because they see something in each other that angers them. However, in any case, the feeling is between two persons and not between a counselor and a client.

Expanded Energy and Decision Making

We often notice that clients find vast stores of unreleased energy. They sleep less, work harder, become more sexually active, and excited about a wider variety of activities. It is as if they took some supercharged vitamins. They begin to experience themselves as dynamic systems that are fueled by their own energy. The more they do the more they are able to do, so it seems.

Likewise, clients sometimes begin to expand the quality and quantity of the decisions they make. Whereas it took someone six weeks to choose to go to school, they now choose a campus, a dorm, a major all in one day. Such clients relish testing out their new found potency.

Spontaneity

Clients in transition are able to live more in the moment. Their mood and behavior is freer, more open, more congruent to the situation. Spontaneous persons reveal themselves to be genuine and transparent in their interpersonal relationships. Such persons are able to express their feelings and do so undefensively and with truth. For them all communication is possible, both the pleasant and hurtful. Further, they act as they feel.

Summary

This chapter centered on the topic of will and the transition point when clients move from the relationship to being-in-the-world. Will, after being stifled by behavioristic and psychoanalytic thought, has again become a subject of concern for counselors, especially existential counselors. Also, will forms a nice vantage point for viewing counseling commitment and client change.

First, counselors who are unable to say "I will help," who are not potent enough to foster change, do their clients a disservice since little movement or growth is possible. Also, they are unable to tolerate the growth and change in clients. Therefore, the point is to create a situation whereby the client can move from counseling to real life, bridge the gap between counseling and life at the transition point.

Six indices of transition were given: 1) changes in language, 2) increased demands on the counselor, 3) dissolution of the technical parameter, 4) increased real feeling, 5) expanded energy and decision making, and 6) increased spontaneity.

GLOSSARY

Tom G. Anderson
California State University
Hayward

A Note on Procedure

This glossary lists and defines some terms commonly encountered in existential literature. The glossary is by no means totally inclusive; it is, however, a good start. First the terms are organized into natural clusters — the order is not alphabetical. Further, the following guides will help the reader in using the glossary: 1) cross-referenced words are in italics; 2) c.f. directs the reader to compare the term in question with the term in parentheses; 3) Syn. is synonym; 4) q.v. means refer to; and 5) unusually used terms are half-quoted, i.e., 'world.'

Set I: Philosophical Foundations

Ontology

Ontology is the study of *Being (Non-Being)* as such, the analysis of the most basic of philosophical questions. Ontology studies the 'ground' or context within which any entity or person can exist; it is thus thinking 'behind' the existence of things. Ontology studies, therefore, those givens of reality prior to (the "Ontological a priori") the existence of anything or anyone. The meanings of *Being-in-the-World* and *Care*, and their unity and inseparateness are the questions of ontology (c.f. *Being-in-the-World, Care, Being and Non-Being*).

Phenomenology

Phenomenology is a process of knowing in which the structure of a phenomenon, idea or experience — the entity-to-be-known — is allowed to 'emerge' from its side as opposed to the knower's side.

Phenomenology is an alternative to, and compromise with, two related processes for knowing: 1) Explanation, which is a transformation via reduction of the entity to a conglomerate of more 'basic' aspects; 2) Phenomenography (from Binswanger), which is an unconstrained, encyclopedic 'swallowing whole' of data. Phenomenology is defined as knowing as 'letting in' of data, but within the context of a priori assumptions (c.f. *'The A Priori,' Existential Analysis*).

Essentialism

Essentialism is the broad approach in philosophy which views forces other than man, or determinitive forces in nature. Human experience is understood as secondary to these idealistic, or naturalistic determinants (c.f. *Existentialism, Cartesian Split*).

Existentialism

Existentialism is the philosophic 'mood' and tendency of movement from generality and abstraction toward the particular and concrete qualities of human experience. Existentialism is 'hostile' toward closed systems of thought; it emphasizes the primacy of the individual person, and the paradoxical-adventurous and the crises-anxiety aspects of living (c.f. *Essentialism*).

'Cartesian Split'

The 'cartesian split' refers to the subject-object dichotomy of traditional philosophy; existentialism attempts to 'cut beneath' the split. Stated another way, existentialism is an alternative to the 'subjective' idealism and the 'objective' realism approaches to philosophy. Idealism explains 'reality' as primarily the consciousness of humans; realism explains 'reality' in terms of the interactions and connections of concrete 'things.' Existentialism describes 'reality' as Being-in-the-World (q.v.); existentialism is a priori idealism or realism. (Syn. subject-object dichotomy; c.f., *Ontology, Essentialism, 'The A Priori.'*)

'The A Priori.'

'The a priori' represents levels of philosophical thought where *'a priori'* refers to 'prior to,' 'the ground for,' 'more basic than,' in the sense that certain understandings are based upon prior ones. The Ontological a priori (Heidegger; q.v., *Ontology*) are studies of *Being (Non-Being)*, and are the most basic of understandings. The Existential a priori (Binswanger; q.v. *Existentialism*) are derived from and based upon the ontologicals; the 'existentials' refer to

studies of the essential qualities of being human (c.f. *Ontology, Existentialism, Being and Non-Being, Being-in-the-World, Care*).

Set II: The Existential Platform

The 'Existential Platform'

The 'existential platform' is a synthesized and general overview of the points of view of many existential philosophers. The 'platform' consists of existential conceptions concerning *systems, individuals, world-views,* and human crises.

The Existential Individual

The existential individual encompasses the existential view which places the particular 'lived' human experience (the 'I-experience') as prior to all else. The existential individual is not only an object of scientific scrutiny or a conglomerate of psychological traits. The existential individual is also not separate from the world, but is in constant interaction with it (c.f. *The Existential Platform, Existentialism, Essentialism*).

Existential 'Systems'

Existential 'systems' are characterized by opposition to 'closed' or essentialistic processes in man, his philosophies and religions, which look primarily to the absolute and eternal, as well as the external, in order to satisfy personal questions as 'who, why, and where am I?' (c.f. *The Existential Platform, Existentialism, Essentialism*).

The Existential World-View

The existential 'world' is constituted by the individual human's interactions with it. The interaction is in three modes of experience: 1) The concrete and natural environment *(Umwelt);* 2) other humans *(Mitwelt);* and 3) the self in relation with itself *(Eigenwelt).* Thus the 'world' of existentialism is not more real than or separate from the individual; it is constituted in the three modes of human existence (c.f. *The Existential Platform*).

Set III: Ultimate States of Existence

Being and Non-Being

These concepts can only be expressed relative to each other, as Being implies Non-Being, and vice-versa. Being is expressed in *Being-in-the-World* (q.v.), whereas Non-Being is expressed in *Care* (q.v.). Being emphasizes the 'is-ness' of existence (Bugental), thus focusing on the individual's existence with things, others and self. Non-Being emphasizes the non-relational aspects, focusing upon the 'nothing,' 'nowhere,' and 'never' givens of existence (c.f. *Ontology, Authenticity, Care, Being-in-the-World*).

Death

Death is understood in existentialism as more than a mere biological event, 'tacked-on' at the end of life. Rather, death is a human, lived experience and the awareness of one's Being-towards-death (*Sein-Sum-Tode,* Heidegger). Death is, in this sense, an awareness of finitude (other than endlessness), contingency (uncontrolledness), and ultimate ownmostness (aloneness). Death is the basis or existential 'given,' which makes tragedy, anxiety, and guilt possible (c.f. *Existential Crisis, Existential Anxiety, Existential Guilt, Being and Non-Being*).

Set IV: Pain

Neurotic Anxiety

Neurotic anxiety tends to be an experience of anticipation of the repetition of earlier trauma. Thus, neurotic anxiety is based primarily upon historical events (i.e., birth trauma is the prototypical 'event' relative to neurotic anxiety). As neurotic anxiety refers to awareness of historically-based repetition of trauma, *existential anxiety* is the future-based anticipation of tragedy and death (c.f. *Existential Anxiety*).

Existential Anxiety

Existential anxiety is the individual's awareness and experience of his own living-in-crisis; i.e., it is the awareness of the ever present possibility for future tragedy in life, or literal *death,* and is a kind of 'ultimate ache.' Existential anxiety is not simply morbid, negative, or pathological, it is appropriate anxiety in the face of reality. Existential anxiety defined as the awareness of reality is not to be cured since it is not pathological. (Syn. *Angst,* c.f. *Existential Crisis, Neurotic Anxiety.*)

Existential Crisis

Crisis refers to the individual's constant existence in the face of his own human limitations where the individual is never fully 'in control' and *existential anxiety* (q.v.) is experienced. Crisis is not to be avoided or 'cured' since it is a given of existence (c.f. *The Existential Platform*).

Existential Guilt

Existential guilt is a human awareness based upon man's limits (his existence toward death). Existential guilt is the sense of unfinishedness or incompleteness; it is the awareness of one's imperfections and human limitations. It is thus a 'given' of existence and is prior to 'derived' guilt, or particular 'guilt feelings' such as feelings of indebtedness to others, or feelings concerning social transgressions. Existential guilt is an awareness in the face of death.

Set V: Modes of Being

Throwness

Thrownness is a human characteristic emphasizing man's 'finding himself' in the world, or as being 'delivered into' his existence. It stresses man's determinedness, the fact that he is created without having been the creator of himself. Thrownness emphasizes man's awareness of himself as a product of his past, in the sense that no human has selected his parents, his brain capacity, race or ethnic origin, or the fact that he is human.

Temporality

Temporality is a basic existential and phenomenological construct which describes human experience in terms of its time 'frame' or temporal reference. Existentialism differentiates temporality from "world or clock time" (Heidegger), the latter being simply measured and sequenced time such as 'past-present-future' and which implies that time 'flows' in a line from 'before' to 'now' to 'after.' Existential temporality is a gestalt, or total unit of experience, where the individual constantly 'lives' his past and future in the present, in the sense that he is always (c.f. *Thrownness, Actualization, Spatiality*).

Spatiality

Spatiality is a basic existential and phenomenological construct which describes human experience in terms of its spatial 'frame' or reference. Existentialism differentiates spatiality from "world space" (Heidegger), the latter being simply measured space, such as the measured direction and distance of concrete entities. Existential spatiality is the human experience of finding and bringing near entities and phenomena. Spatiality (as well as *Temporality,* q.v.) belies the Cartesian simplicity that 'man is in space' or that 'space is in man' (c.f. *Cartesian Split, Temporality*).

Being-in-the-World

Being-in-the-world is the broad concept which states the interaction and inseparability of man and 'the world.' Being-in-the-World describes human modes, experiences, and conditions of the person's being-with (constituting) other entities, other persons and with one's self. Being-in-the-World 'cuts beneath' and is more generic than the traditional philosophical subject-object dichotomy. Being-in-the-World along with *Care* (q.v.) is one of the Ontological a priori (c.f. *'The A Priori,' The Cartesian Split, Care*).

Set VI: Positive Goals

'Self'

'Self' is a quality of human existence which is authentic and antithetical to alienated or fallen *'They'* (q.v.). 'Self' is aware of nonexistence within its existence. 'Self' is characterized as that which is silent as opposed to 'chattering' which 'tarries alongside' entities (Heidegger). Self is an awareness of its own Non-Being (c.f. *'They,' Authenticity, Fallenness, Care*).

Authenticity

Authenticity is the quality of human existence which is potentially actualizable. Authenticity is 'caringly being-in-the-world' in that the individual in being-with entities, others and self *(Being in-the-World)*, is aware simultaneously of his 'ownmostness,' his limits and his ultimate non-existence. Authenticity entails not losing the 'perspective' that existence is conditioned by non-existence (c.f. *Actualization, Existential Psychotherapy, Fallenness, 'They'*).

Care

Care describes human modes, experiences and conditions of the person's being aware of his ultimate and unique — his 'ownmost' — non-existence. Care expresses the antithesis of existence. It is a broad, basic, idea which is in itself non-reducible to more 'basic' understandings, and is thus an Ontological a priori. Care is antithetical to, yet inseparable from, *Being-in-the World*. Where Being-in-the-World expresses man's being with things, others, and self, Care expresses man's not being-with; his non-existence (q.v. *'The A Priori'*; c.f. *Ontology, Being-in-the-World, Being and Non-Being*).

Actualization

Actualization is the realization of potentials. In counseling, the term implies that the counselor assumes that his client has latent abilities or awarenesses which can become manifest and functional.

Set VII: Negative Goals

Fallenness

Fallenness is a dynamic process, or movement, where the individual becomes more or less 'captive' to, or enticed by the world of material things, and other people, or *'They'* (q.v.). The fallen person is inauthentic in that he, in falling, has traded himself for *'They'* (c.f. *'They,' Authenticity*).

'They'

'They' is a quality of human existence meaning to exist as *Das Man* (Heidegger) where the *'Self'* (q.v.) is traded off (or alienated) to the 'masses.' 'They's' existence is characterized as 'everyday' averageness, as safety and comfortableness. 'They' does not 'stand out.' Further 'they' is palliative and enticing as 'they' does not face the awareness of non-existence as tragedy or *Death*; i.e., 'They' does not *Care*, and is the individual's way of inauthenticity (c.f. *Authenticity, Fallenness, Care, Death, 'Self'*).

Set VIII: Existential Therapy

Principles of the Existential Psychotherapy Relationship

The principles place primary emphasis on the client's experiencing of his existence, where the counselor, as 'existential,' adheres to the tenets that 1) the relationship is not instrumental or technical; 2) it focuses on the client-as-self; 3) 'Presence' is emphasized on its various meanings; and 4) client-crises are experienced as opposed to 'cured' (c.f. *Existential Psychotherapy*).

Encounter

Encounter is a dialogue in which persons are authentically present to one another, and where they are both changed. Encounter establishes a "moment of vision" (Heidegger), which implies to 'make present' in the 'here-and-now' by a resolute reflection and awaiting. Implicit in encounter is its unpredictability (and amazement); its transcendence in the sense of 'making present' the spatial 'there' and temporal 'then'; and where dialogue is between 'self and self' not 'they and they' (c.f. *Existential Psychotherapy, Authenticity, 'Self', 'They', Temporality, Spatiality*).

Existential Psychotherapy

Existential Psychotherapy is a broad counseling approach which employs the concepts of existentialism in order to understand and communicate the nature of the counselor-client relationship. The *Principles of the Existential Psychotherapy Relationship* (q.v.) are generally adhered to, however Existential Psychotherapy may not represent standardized counseling methodology (c.f. *Existential Analysis*).

Existential Analysis

Existential analysis is a reconstruction of the inner world of clients, where existential concepts provide the framework for understanding the client. Psychoanalytic methodology is often employed in existential analytic counseling. Existential analysis is thus a synthesis of existential concepts, psychoanalytic methodology and *Phenomenology* (Syn. *Daseinanalyse;* c.f. *Existential Psychotherapy, Phenomenology*).

BIBLIOGRAPHY

Allport, G. *Letters from Jenny.* New York: Harcourt, Brace and World, 1965.
Alschuler, A. Psychological education. *Journal of Humanistic Psychology,* 1969, 9, pp. 1-17.
Arbuckle, D. *Counseling: An introduction.* Boston: Allyn and Bacon, 1961.
———. *Counseling and psychotherapy: An overview.* New York: McGraw-Hill, 1967.
———. *Counseling: Philosophy, theory and practice.* Boston: Allyn and Bacon, 1965.
Assagioli, R. *The act of will.* New York: Viking Press, 1973.
———. *The training of the will.* New York: Psychosynthesis Research Foundation, 1966.
Aubrey, R. In book review (*Counseling: Philosophy, theory, and practice,* by Dugald Arbuckle). *Personnel and Guidance Journal,* June, 1971, 49, 10, p. 848.
Back, K. Can subjects be human and humans be subjects?, in J. Criswell, H. Soloman, and P. Suppes (Eds.), *Mathematical methods in small group process.* Stanford, Cal.: Stanford Press, 1962, pp. 35-48.
Banikiotes, P. A preventive approach to mental health in the schools. *Counseling and Values,* 1973, 2, 112-117.
Barclay, J. *Foundations of counseling strategies.* New York: Wiley, 1971.
Barrett, W. *Irrational man: A study in existential philosophy.* New York: Doubleday, 1962.
Beck, C. *Guidelines for guidance: Readings in the philosophy of guidance.* Dubuque, Iowa: William C. Brown, 1966.
———. *Philosophical foundations of guidance.* Englewood Cliffs, New Jersey: Prentice-Hall, 1963.
Bennis, W., Benne, L. K., and Chin, R., *Changing organizations.* New York: McGraw-Hill, 1966.
———. *The planning of change.* New York: Holt, Rinehart, and Winston, 1969.
Binswanger, L. *Being-in-the-world.* New York: Basic Books, 1963.
Blake, R. and Mouton, J. *The managerial grid.* Houston: The Gulf Publishing Co., 1961.

Blocher, D. and Shaffer, W. Guidance and human development, in D. Cooks, *Guidance for education in revolution*. Boston: Allyn and Bacon, 1971, pp. 90–117.

Bonner, H. The proactive personality, in J. Bugental (Ed.), *Challenges of humanistic psychology*. New York: McGraw-Hill, 1967.

Boss, M. "Daseinanalysis" and psychotherapy, in T. Millon (Ed.), *Theories of psychopathology*. Philadelphia: W. B. Saunders, 1967.

Boyatzis, R. Building efficacy: An effective use of managerial power. *Industrial Management Review*, 1969, *11*, pp. 65–77.

Brammer, L. and Shostrom, E. *Therapeutic psychology: Fundamentals of actualization counseling and psychotherapy*. Englewood Cliffs, New Jersey: Prentice-Hall, 1968.

Bugental, J. The challenge that is man, in Bugental (Ed.), *Challenges of humanistic psychology*. New York: McGraw-Hill, 1967.

———. *The search for authenticity*. New York: Holt, Rinehart, and Winston, 1965.

Buhler, C. Basic theoretical concepts of humanistic psychology. *American Psychologist*, 1971, *26*, pp. 378–386.

———. *Der menschliche lebenslauf als psychologisches problem* (The human cause of life as a psychological problem). Leipzig: Hirzel, 1933.

———. and Massarik, F. *The course of human life: A study of goals in humanistic perspective*. New York: Springer, 1968.

Burton, A. *Twelve therapists*. San Francisco: Jossey-Bass, 1972.

Caplan, G. *Principles of preventive psychiatry*. New York: Basic Books, 1964.

Chenault, J. Syntony: A philosophical premise for theory and research. *Journal of Humanistic Psychology*, 1966, pp. 31–36.

Corlis, R. and Rabe, P. *Psychotherapy from the center: A humanistic view of change and growth*. Scranton, Pa.: International Textbook Co., 1969.

Corsini, R. Issues in encounter groups: Comments on Coulson's article, *The Counseling Psychologist*, 1971, pp. 28–38.

Coulson, W. and Rogers, C. *Man and the science of man*. Columbus, Ohio: Merrill, 1968.

Crapo, S. Counselor trainee stylized behavior. Unpublished manuscript, California State University, Hayward, 1971.

Cronbach, L. and Meehl, P. Construct validity in psychological tests. *Psychol. Bull.*, 1955, *52*, pp. 281–301.

Dailey, C. *Assessment of lives*. San Francisco: Jossey-Bass, 1971.

Denney, R. and Sydow, F. Issac Newton's unfortunate fall. *Change*, 1973, *4*, pp. 55–60.

Dinkmeyer, D. The counselor as a consultant: Rationale and procedures. *Elementary School Guidance and Counseling*, 1968, *2*, pp. 187–194.

Durant, W. and Durant, A. *The lessons of history*. New York: Simon and Schuster, 1968.

Ellis, A. *Reason in emotion and psychotherapy.* New York: Lyle Stuart, 1962.

Erikson, E. *Childhood and society.* New York: Norton, 1963.

Faust, V. *The counselor-consultant in the elementary school.* Boston: Houghton Mifflin, 1968.

Ferenczi, S. *Further contributions to the theory and technique of psychoanalysis.* New York: Basic Books, 1950.

Ford, D. and Urban, H. *Systems of psychotherapy: A comparative study.* New York: Wiley, 1965.

Frankl, V. *The doctor and the soul.* New York: Knopf, 1955.

———. *Man's search for meaning: An introduction to logotherapy.* New York: Washington Square Press, 1963.

———. *Psychotherapy and existentialism: Selected papers on logotherapy.* New York: Simon and Schuster, 1967.

———. *The will to meaning: Foundations and applications of logotherapy.* New York, Plume Books, 1969.

Frey, D. Being systematic when you have but one subject: Idiographic method, N = 1, and all that. *Measurement and Evaluation in Guidance,* April, 1973, Vol. 6, 2, pp. 39–44.

———. Conceptualizing counseling theories: A content analysis of process and goal statements. *Counselor Education and Supervision,* 1972, *11,* pp. 243–250.

———. The counselor and change: A tie that binds. *CPGA Journal,* 1971, *4,* pp. 38–41.

———. and Conyne, R. Group process teaching and the live case study approach. *Counselor Education and Supervision,* 1972, *11,* pp. 73–75.

Getzels, J. and Thelen, H. The classroom as a unique social system, in *Fifty-Ninth Yearb. Nat. Soc. Stud. Educ.* (Part III). Chicago: University of Chicago Press, 1960, pp. 53–82.

Gibb, J. The counselor as a role-free person, in C. Parker (Ed.), *Counseling theories and counselor education.* Boston: Houghton Mifflin, 1968.

———. Role freedom in a TORI group, in A. Burton (Ed.), *Encounter: The theory and practice of encounter groups.* San Francisco: Jossey-Bass Co., 1969.

———. TORI Community. Unpublished manuscript, Center for The Study of the Person, La Jolla, California, 1970.

Goble, F. *The third force: Psychology and Abraham Maslow.* New York: Grossman, 1970.

Halleck, S. You can go to hell with style. *Psychology Today,* November, 1969, *3,* p. 16.

Harper, R. *Psychoanalysis and psychotherapy: 36 systems.* Englewood Cliffs, N. J.: Prentice-Hall, 1959.

Hunt, J. McV. *Intelligence and experience.* Boston: Ronald Press, 1960.

Ivey, A. and Weinstein, G. The counselor as a specialist in psychological education (a dialogue). *Personnel and Guidance Journal,* 1970, *49,* pp. 98–107.

Johnson, R. *Existential man: The challenge of psychotherapy.* New York: Pergamon Press, 1971.

Jourard, S. and Overlade, D. *Reconciliation: A theory of man transcending* (From the work of Franklin J. Shaw [Dec.]). Princeton, N. J.: Van Nostrand Co., 1966.

Kagan, N., Krathwohl, D., and Farquhar, W. *IPR interpersonal process recall: Simulated recall by videotape.* Educational Research Series, No. 24, East Lansing: College of Education, Michigan State University, 1965, 111-1 to 111-22.

Kehas, C. Toward a redefinition of education: A new framework for counseling in education, in B. Shertzer and S. Stone (Eds.), *Introduction to guidance: Selected readings.* Boston: Houghton Mifflin, 1970, pp. 59–71.

Kelly, G. Humanistic methodology in psychological research, in B. Maher's (Ed.), *Clinical psychology and personality: The selected papers of George Kelly.* New York: Wiley, 1969.

———. *The psychology of personal constructs.* Vol. 1 *A theory of personality.* New York: Norton, 1955.

Kemp, C. G. Existential counseling. *The Counseling Psychologist,* 1971, *2,* pp. 2–29.

———. *Intangibles in counseling.* Boston: Houghton Mifflin, 1967.

Kohlberg, L. and Mayer, R. Development as an aim of education. *Harvard Educational Review,* 1972, *42,* pp. 449–496.

Laing, R. *The politics of experience.* New York: Ballantine Books, 1967.

Lirette, H. The concept of change in Gabriel Marcel and Rollo May: Implications for counseling. Unpublished master's thesis, California State University, Hayward, 1972.

London, P. *The modes and morals of psychotherapy.* New York: Holt, Rinehart, and Winston, 1964.

Mahrer, A. *The goals of psychotherapy.* New York: Appleton-Century-Crofts, 1967.

Malcolm, D. On becoming a counselor. *Personnel and Guidance,* 1968, *47,* pp. 673–676.

Maslow, A. *Eupsychian management.* Illinois: Irwin-Dorsey, 1965.

———. *Motivation and personality.* New York: Harper and Row, 1954.

———. A philosophy of psychology: The need for a mature science of human nature. *Main Currents in Modern Thought.* 1955, *13,* 27–32.

———. *Religions, values, and peak experiences.* Columbus, Ohio: Ohio State University Press, 1964.

———. A theory of human maturation, in L. Gorlow and W. Katkowsky (Eds.), *Readings in the psychology of adjustment.* New York: McGraw-Hill, 1959.

———. *Toward a psychology of being.* Princeton, N. J.: Van Nostrand, 1962.

———. *The psychology of science: A reconnaissance.* New York: Harper and Row, 1966.

May, R. *Existential psychology.* New York: Random House, 1960.

———. *Love and will.* New York: Norton, 1969.

———. *Man's search for himself.* New York: Norton, 1953.

———. *The meaning of anxiety.* New York: Norton, 1950.

———. *Power and innocence.* New York: Norton, 1971.

———. *Psychology and the human dilemma.* Princeton, N.J.: Van Nostrand, 1967.

———., Angel, E. and Ellenberger, H. *Existence: A new dimension in psychiatry and psychology.* New York: Basic Books, 1958.

McCully, C. The counselor: Instrument of change. *Teachers College Record,* 66, 1965.

———. and Miller, L. *Challenge for change in counselor education.* Minneapolis: Burgess, 1969.

Meehl, P. Symposium on clinical and statistical prediction: The tie that binds. *J. counsel. Psychol.,* 1956, 3, p. 163.

Mogar, R. Toward a psychological theory of education. *Journal of Humanistic Psychology,* 1969, 9, pp. 17–52.

Mosher, R. and Sprinthall, N. Psychological education in secondary schools: A program to promote individual and human development. *Amer. Psychologist,* 1970, 25, pp. 911–924.

Patterson, C. *Theories of counseling and psychotherapy.* New York: Harper and Row, 1966.

———. What is counseling psychology? *J. counsel. Psychol.,* 1969, 16, pp. 23–29.

Perls, F. *Ego, hunger, and aggression.* London: George Allen and Unwin, 1947.

———., Hefferline, R., and Goodman, P. *Gestalt therapy: Excitement and growth in the human personality.* New York: Julien Press, 1951.

———. *Gestalt therapy verbatim.* Lafayette, California: Real People Press, 1969.

———. *In and out of the garbage pail.* Lafayette, California: Real People Press, 1969.

Raming, H. and Frey, D. A taxonomic approach to the Gestalt theory of Perls. *J. counsel. Psychol.,* 1974, 22, pp. 179–184.

Reinhardt, K. *The existential revolt: The main themes and phases of existentialism.* New York: Ungar Publishers, 1960.

Rogers, C. *Carl Rogers on encounter groups.* New York: Harper and Row, 1970.

———. *Client-centered counseling.* Boston: Houghton Mifflin, 1951.

———. *The clinical treatment of the problem child.* Boston: Houghton Mifflin, 1939.

———. *Counseling and psychotherapy.* Boston: Houghton Mifflin, 1942.

———. *On becoming a person.* Boston: Houghton Mifflin, 1961.

Rosso, S. and Frey, D. An assessment of the gap between counseling theory and practice. *J. counsel. Psychol.*, 1973, *20*, pp. 471–476.

Rychlak, J. *Introduction to personality and psychotherapy: A theory construction approach.* Boston: Houghton Mifflin, 1973.

Sahakian, W. *Psychotherapy and counseling: Studies in technique.* Chicago: Rand McNally, 1969.

Shaw, F. Counseling, in P. Farnsworth (Ed.), *Annual review of psychology.* Palo Alto: Annual Review, Inc., 1957.

Shertzer, B. and Stone, S. *Fundamentals of counseling*, 2nd Edition. Boston: Houghton Mifflin, 1974.

Skinner, B. F. *Beyond freedom and dignity.* New York: Knopf, 1971.

Snygg, D. and Combs, A. *Individual behavior: A new frame of reference for psychology.* New York: Harper and Row, 1949.

Stubbins, J. The politics of counseling. *Personnel and Guidance Journal*, 1970, *48*, pp. 611–618.

Super, D. *The psychology of careers.* New York: Harper and Row, 1957.

Swensen, C. *An approach to case conceptualization*, in S. Stone and B. Shertzer (Eds.), Guidance Monograph Series. Boston: Houghton Mifflin, Co., 1968.

Thoreson, C. Behavioral humanism. Unpublished manuscript, Stanford University, 1972.

Tyler, L. Design for a hopeful psychology. *Amer. Psychologist*, *28*, December, 1973, pp. 1021–1029.

———. *The work of the counselor.* New York: Appleton-Century-Crofts, 1969.

van Kaam, A. Counseling and psychotherapy from the viewpoint of existential psychology, in D. Arbuckle (Ed.), *Counseling and psychotherapy: An overview.* New York: McGraw-Hill, 1967.

———. The goals of psychotherapy from the existential point of view, in Mahrer (Ed.), *The goals of psychotherapy.* New York: Appleton-Century-Crofts, 1967, pp. 145–161.

Wheelis, A. *The desert.* New York: Harper and Row, 1969.

———. *The quest for identity.* New York: Norton, 1958.

Wilson, C. *New pathways in psychology: Maslow and the post-Freudian revolution.* New York: Taplinger, 1972.

Winthrop, H. Existentialism and phenomenological frontiers. *Journal of Existentialism*, 1966, *6*, pp. 343–354.

INDEX

A priori, 84
Action-affect counseling, 9
Action-rational counseling, 9
Actualization, 89
Affect, 25
Allport, G., 64
Alschuler, A., 56
Anderson, T., 83
Anxiety
    existential, 86
    general, 27
    neurotic, 86
Arbuckle, D., 20
Assagioli, R., 75
Assessment, 60
Aubrey, R., 37
Authenticity
    conflict, 41
    guilt, 39
    positive, 88
Back, K., 66
Banikiotes, P., 55
Barclay, J., 74
Barrett, W., 4, 11
Beck, C., 13, 20, 23
Being, 26, 83, 85
Being-in-the-world, 29, 88
Benne, K., 56
Bennis, W., 56
Binswanger, L., 13
Blake, R., 56
Blocher, D., 64
Bonner, H., 6
Boss, M., 13–14
Boyatzis, R., 56
Brammer, L., 51
Bugental, J., 18, 22
Buhler, C., 64
Burton, A., 16
Caplan, G., 55
Care, 88
Cartesian split, 84
Change, 75

Chenault, J., 58
Chin, R., 56
Choice, 29
Client
    demands, 80
    needs, 48
Combs, A., 23
Commitment, 42
Consultation, 55
Contact, 25
Conyne, R., 70
Corlis, R., 47
Corsini, R., 31
Crapo, S., 49
Crisis, 86
Cronbach, L., 69
Dailey, C., 64
Data
    collection, 61
    "inside the skin," 68
    "outside the skin," 67
Death, 27, 86
Decision making, 80
Denney, R., 63
Daseinanalysis, 13–14, 26
Dinkmeyer, D., 55
Durant, A., xi
Durant, W., xi
Eigenwelt, 29
Ellis, A., 63
Encounter, 24, 44, 89
Energy, 80
Epistemology, 67
Erikson, E., 64
Essentialism, 84
Existence, 26, 40, 85
Existential
    aggregate, 1
    analysis, 90
    counseling, 5–6
    individual, 85
    platform, 85
    psychotherapy, 90

Existential — continued
  system, 85
  therapy, 89
  world view, 85
Existentialism
  definition, 84
  history of, 11
Existentialists
  in the healing arts, 12
Experiential parameter, 63
External press, 57
Fallenness, 89
Faust, V., 55
Feeling, 80
Ferenczi, S., 73
Flexibility, 40, 49
Ford, D., 48
Frankl, V., 14, 28, 75
Freedom, 30
Frey, D., 5, 7, 17, 31, 54, 66, 69, 70, 75
Getzels, J., 37
Gibb, J., 56
Gilmore, S., 65–66
Goals
  client, 34
  counseling, 33
  counselor, 36
  existential, 39
  institution, 37
  negative, 89
  positive, 88
  process, 38
  universal, 38
Goble, F., 17
Guilt, 87
Halleck, S., 49
Harper, R., 7
Hemingway, E., 4
"Here and now," 25
Honesty, 41
Humanistic movement, 21
Hunt, J., 68
Husserl, E., 23
Impact, 3
Imperfection, 50
Implementation, 53
Intentionality, 30
Internal qualities, 57
Intervention, 53
Insight-affect counseling, 9
Insight-rational counseling, 9
Introgression, 53
Ivey, A., 56
Johnson, R., 47
Jourard, S., 58
Joy, 28
Kagan, N., 67

Kelly, G., 63, 64, 69
Kemp, C., 5, 19, 48
Kierkegaard, S., 11
Kohlberg, L., 67
Laing, R., 9
Language, 79
Liberation, 40
Lirette, H., 15
Live case method, 70
London, P., 7
Mahrer, A., 38
Malcolm, D., 51–54
Maslow, A., 17, 57, 64
Massarik, F., 64
May, R., 5, 14, 30, 45, 56, 75, 76
Mayer, R., 67
McCully, H., 19
Meaning, 28
Meehl, P., 61, 69
Miller, L., 19
Mitwelt, 29
Mogar, R., 56
Mosher, R., 56
Moulton, J., 56
Mutuality, 24
N=1, 64
Narrow philosophy, 57
Nietzsche, F., 11
Non-being, 26
Ontological a priori, 83
Ontology, 83
Overlade, D., 58
Pain, 27, 86
Patterson, C., 8, 46, 55–56
Perls, F., 16, 25
Person/environment dimension, 54
Person/person dimension, 53
Phenomenology, 22, 83
Philosophic parameter, 62
Philosophical foundations, 83
Post-hoc definition, 49
Potency, 75
Power, 56
Process, 26
Rabe, R., 47
Raming, H., 5, 17
Reconciliation theory, 58
Research, 54
Rienhardt, K., 15
Rogers, C., 15, 23
Rosso, S., 5, 67
Rychlak, J., 13, 23
Sahakian, W., 23
Sartre, J., 12
Self
  acceptance, 42
  definition, 31, 88

Shaffer, W., 64
Shaw, F., 58
Shertzer, B., 25, 50
Shostrom, E., 51
Skinner, B., 33, 67
Snygg, D., 23
Spatiality, 87
Spontaneity, 81
Sprinthall, N., 56
Stone, S., 25, 50
Structure, 50
Stubbins, J., 56
Stylized behavior, 49
Super, D., 64
Swensen, C., 64
Sydow, F., 63
Syntony, 58
Tangibility, 3
Technical parameter, 66, 80

Technique, 44–45
Temporality, 87
Thelen, H., 37
"They," 89
"Third force," 22
Thoreson, C., 9
Thrownness, 87
Transition, 77
Tyler, L., 66, 70
Umwelt, 29
Understanding, 48
Urban, D., 48
Validation, 69
van Kaam, A., 6, 24, 39
Weinstein, G., 56
Wheelis, A., 28, 30, 74–75
Will, 31, 73
Wilson, C., 17, 74–75
Winthrop, H., 49